THE
Empress
OF Victoria

BY GODFREY HOLLOWAY

acknowledgements

Just as the reputation of The Empress represents the efforts of many dedicated people so this book reflects the interest and affection of dozens of people who have passed on to us their memories and experiences within the walls of what has become a Canadian monument to the nostalgia of a gracious era.

To mention all the names of these friendly people would double the size of this book, but it is hoped they will find consolation within these pages even if their contributions can be read only between the lines.

Acknowledgement should also be made to The Empress staff whose lively interest in the progress of the book was a continuing encouragement.

This history of The Empress hotel in Victoria British Columbia was first published in 1969. Since that time the hotel has been subjected to several refurbishments and a massive restoration and this little book has achieved "best seller" status. It was deemed appropriate that it too, should undergo a degree of renovation and expansion.

There may be passages in the text which were authentic at the period to which they apply but could appear contradictory in later sequences.

To my Wife
Who graciously took second place
during my affair with The Empress

Published by Key Pacific Publishers Co. Ltd., Third floor, 1001 Wharf Street, Victoria, B.C. V8W 1T6, in cooperation with The Empress Group. Lithographed in Canada by Hemlock Printers Ltd. ISBN 1-895114-00-4 Copyright Canada 1980-Godfrey Holloway, Copyright Canada 1989-The Empress Group. All rights reserved. No part of this book may be reproduced in any form without permission in writing from The Publisher. The Empress of Victoria was first published in 1968, revised in 1976, updated for a third printing in 1980 and reprinted in 1984 and 1986. After major renovations to the hotel in 1988-89 the book required amendment and addition for reprinting in 1989.

Contents

Cover: *The bronze casting of the British Royal Crown can be seen in the centre of the gallery in the new Reception Pavilion of the hotel. This heraldic crown is copied from the original bejewelled crown fashioned for the reign of Queen Elizabeth II.*

Painting by Aubiniere (1887) shows area behind the old James Bay bridge where The Empress now stands. Buildings in the rear include Pendray's soap works and Wyler's furniture store.

Chapter 1

721 Government Street

"I don't believe it is going too far to call The Empress the pet hotel of the British Empire."

Sir Alexander Gibb, CBE

In a very special way, The Empress is Victoria. The reverse, too, is true: Victoria is The Empress.

The two are linked in a way extremely few other hotels and their cities have ever been. Photographers "shooting" Victoria inevitably end up with the Inner Harbor area, dominated by The Empress and the provincial legislative buildings. People suggesting a rendezvous are more than likely to name The Empress lobby. A night out in Victoria becomes something special if it includes dinner at The Empress. Convention in Victoria? Where else but The Empress? Especially now that the magnificent new Victoria Conference Centre has become attached to the hotel.

The big vine-covered pile of brick and the gorgeous gardens surrounding it seem not to be a commercial enterprise so much as a civic development. And while the spanking new hotels and motels that have mushroomed throughout the city are undoubtedly a matter of economic concern to The Empress, they are after all just hotels. They are not The Empress. They lack affection.

Affection does seem to be the key word. People poke fun at The Empress. They chuckle over the potted palms. They shake their heads at the conservatory. They laugh uproariously at the mammoth halls and corridors.

But they do so with affection.

Truth is, they love The Empress. They love its potted palms. They wept when Billy Tickle retired. They are enthralled by the lobby and the Palm Court, the Crystal Ballroom and the beautifully expanded gardens.

The Empress draws upon an enormous well of good will. And all those uncounted people around the world who love The Empress watched with warm delight and a little anxiety as the renovation of the 1960's, "Operation Teacup", eased its way into providing more streamlined amenities.

These people knew that if The Empress was to survive in today's world it must be more up to date than it had been. They desperately wanted The Empress to survive. There had even been rumors of demolition. Horrors!

If The Empress were to become too utterly modern the pastiche would be gone. The Empress must somehow be modern without seeming so and its well-wishers were relieved to find this is exactly what "Operation Teacup" achieved. The Empress became if not a red-hot momma, at least a dowager with a difference.

The bright girl with the mini-skirt, is bound to attract attention. But get a roomful of them and there is a depressing similarity. It matters little which one ends up on your lap.

Introduce an older woman into such a crowd. One who is alive and eager, tuned in. It is obvious that experience counts, that beauty cared for beyond the first flush of youth is the more alluring beauty, that - well, sophistication and good manners and a real knowledge of how the world works, enable such a woman to meet and overwhelm without effort the frantic yet basically identical competition of the young swingers.

Add to this the mature ability to be a little bit different and you have a woman with whom the hip crowd simply cannot compete.

And to the great relief of all those who have been in love with her for these many years, this is what The Empress has become after a good going over costing some $6 million in 1967 and a complete renovation in 1989 costing close to $50 million. Furthermore there will be a continuing programme of refurbishing the refurbished.

Before the hotel was built there had been considerable discussion regarding the site selected by Sir Thomas Shaughnessy, president of Canadian Pacific Railway.

From an engineer's point of view a low lying tidal swamp was less than impressive. But the president could visualize a fine hotel set back from a massive stone seawall with paved streets, rose gardens, lawns and trees creating a unique harborside spectacle.

The president's choice prevailed and in July 1904 outstanding foundation engineers submitted their recommendations and stated if followed the building would be absolutely safe.

The hotel is resting on what might best be described as a massive crumpet made of Victoria yellow and blue clay with 3,353 piles, 60,500 FBM of planking and timbers for coffer dams and 9,000 cubic yards of concrete.

Ever since 1912 records of levels have been kept on any settlement or movement of the structure, but in over 80 years the old lady has only settled 30 inches (75 cm) from north to south and it is doubtful whether any casual visitor would even notice.

The hotel is as safe this afternoon as tea and crumpets are being served, as the opening day.

At 721 Government Street she is now the dowager who is with it.

(Upper left) Francis M. Rattenbury, architecture for The Empress. (Below left) George Henry Barnard became mayor of Victoria in order to develop his idea for a first-class hotel. (Upper right) J.W. Troup (L) accepted S.S. Princess Kathleen at Clydebank, Scotland with a C.P. official. (Bottom) The interior of one of the Princess steamers, circa 1912.

chapter 2

The Grand Vision

"...the first big tourism promoters on the west coast of Canada"

As the last echoes of the 19th century were fading away, two men in Victoria sold a grand vision to the Canadian Pacific Railway. Out of their dream grew both The Empress Hotel and the famous fleet of Princess ferries.

One of the two men was Capt. J.W. Troup, a former sternwheeler master from the Columbia River. The other was George Henry Barnard, a lawyer whose father had operated the famous Barnard Express to the Cariboo during the British Columbia gold rush of the 1860's.

It might even be said that these two men were the first big tourism promoters on the west coast of Canada.

They looked at the Pacific Coast of North America, from Los Angeles to the Alaska Panhandle, as a vast potential playground. To their minds, Vancouver Island was the kingpin. And the key to Vancouver Island was a fast ferry service from the mainland to Victoria plus a deluxe hotel for the travellers when they got there.

Victoria, at that time a city of only 25,000 people, already had a reputation for fine hotels. Best on the Pacific Coast, some said.

What "some" said didn't matter.

Troup took off to Montreal where he convinced the CPR to build a fast ferry and was himself commissioned to go to England and have her built. That was the first *Princess Victoria*, which during its years of faithful service became popularly known as "Old Vic".

Meanwhile, back in Victoria, Barnard raised howls of sarcastic glee when he first suggested his scheme, the main point

The old James Bay Bridge (above) was replaced with a stone causeway. The Empress was built on a swampy area behind the bridge. (Below) The hotel under construction in 1907.

of which consisted of building a causeway across James Bay and filling in the flats behind with mud dredged from the harbor plus thousands of yards of gravel. Then he proposed driving piles 125 feet through this fill for a foundation on which to build a 160-room hotel.

Barnard figured the city should make some concessions and to ensure it did he got himself elected to the city council in 1902. Two years later he won a two-year term as mayor. That was all the time he needed.

On August 24, 1903, alderman Lawrence Goodacre, a local butcher, moved that the city enter an agreement with the CPR "for the erection of a tourist hotel at James Bay and to grant certain lands and exemptions in consideration thereof". The motion was seconded by Alderman Alex Stewart, a stone-cutter, who had his business alongside Ross Bay Cemetery.

Three weeks later the taxpayers passed the bylaw by a healthy majority. On July 7, 1904, following strenuous support from Mayor Barnard, the citizens voted 1,205 to 46 in favor of granting certain tax exemptions to the CPR.

Within two weeks the big hotel was underway and, although the agreement with the city called for a structure worth at least $300,000, the actual costs rose to more than $1.6 million.

·The hotel was designed by Francis Mawson Rattenbury, an English architect who had moved to Victoria in 1893 after winning a fortune in northern gold rushes. In England he had designed the entire model town of Saltaire. In Victoria he also designed the British Columbia legislative buildings across the Inner Harbor from The Empress as well as the Bank of Montreal Building on Government Street and two successive Canadian Pacific Railway depots on Government Street, the first of brown shingles, the second of stone. Other Victoria buildings designed by Rattenbury are The Crystal Garden and CPR Steamship office in association with Leonard James and, with Sam Maclure, the second Government House which burned down in 1957. His influence even extended across the Strait of Georgia, where he designed the Vancouver Court House and the old Hotel Vancouver.

The Empress did not rise overnight. In that era of hand labor and horse-drawn wagons, it took four years for contractor J.L.

A group of local officials and press gather on the steps of The Empress to welcome the arrival of Canadian Pacific S.S. Empress of Russia, *June 1913. Hotel Manager H. Jackson is in the front row on the right. (Below) S.S.* Princess Marguerite *made a daily round trip from Seattle during the summer months for many years. She has been replaced by more modern vessels. (Bob Stocks photo)*

Skene to erect the stately hostelry, with walls of the ground floor 30 inches thick and great wood beams criss-crossed under the roof to give the apex of the original building the appearance of a fortress.

Eventually, however, the job was done, and on January 20, 1908, the first guests signed the register of The Empress Hotel, and packed its 116 guest rooms.

And what a scene greeted their eyes! With interior decorating the work of Mrs. Hayter Reed, whose husband was superintendent of Canadian Pacific Hotels at the time, The Empress was said to be "beautiful in its magnificent stateliness" on opening day. That first night, dinner was served at 7 p.m. to a fashionable crowd gathered in formal dress in the dining room whose tinted walls and ornate ceiling have since graced so many grand affairs down through the years.

What of those who created The Empress?

Troup continued building up the Princess fleet. Soon the famous Triangle Run was serving Vancouver, Victoria and Seattle with the midnight boat between Vancouver and Victoria carrying many businessmen and politicians, as well as countless newlyweds.

(The fleet's brand of old world luxury travel no longer fitted the modern age. The *Princess Marguerite*, which brought summer tourists from Seattle to the hotel's doorstep in the Inner Harbor, was sold in 1975, to the Government of British Columbia. She was re-vamped and modernized. With a Union Jack painted across her stern she became a floating tourist attraction until she was again sold, in 1989, to BC Stena Line who found the Maggie unable to compete with developing competition such as catamarans, which do the trip in half the time, and her more modern sister ship *Vancouver Island Princess* which plies the same route.

Larger and modern ships capable of carrying buses, RVs, campers and cars will handle the increasing tourist traffic and perhaps reintroduce Captain Troup's turn-of-the-century idea of a triangle route connecting Victoria with Seattle and Vancouver. These ships, however, will have the added attraction of slot machines.)

Barnard pressed on in his political career, became Victoria's member of Parliament and later was sent to the Senate from

(Top) The Empress is a focal point in the grand parade of 1912, celebrating the coronation of King George V (Empress Archives). (Bottom left) A former symbol of Victoria was its "English-type" bobby. The present symbol is the cluster lamppost and hanging flower baskets (bottom right).

which he resigned when he felt too old for further service to his country. A most unusual gesture which some of our present sentors might emulate. (Service was a strong-point with the Barnard family. His brother Frank was one time Lieutenant-Governor of British Columbia and was knighted for his services during the First World War.)

And poor Francis Rattenbury, the architect, returned to England with his second wife, Alma Victoria, many years his junior. An emotionally unstable woman, she was a heavy drinker with a strong sexual appetite. The Rattenburys' 20 year old chauffeur became Alma Victoria's lover and in the 1930's both stood trial in England for the murder of Francis Rattenbury. The court case was highly publicized in England and Victoria and became a successful play and film by Graham Greene.

Nor did The Empress Rattenbury designed remain long unchanged. Within two years of its historic debut, a north wing was added, containing 85 rooms and a library which became the Coronet Room, and now The Bengal Room. In 1929, just as the depression clouded the world, the so-called New Wing was added on Humboldt Street, containing 270 rooms and suites, thus raising the total to 416 rooms.

Nature had a final fling at The Empress when the New Wing was built. It was found impossible to locate a footing for the two foundations where the new wing was to join the old, therefore it became necessary to build the bridge that arches between the two buildings over what once was a stream flowing beside the Church of Our Lord to the Inner Harbor.*

So The Empress stands today, outwardly at least. Romance has grown around her, legends lurk in many of her crannies and 12-foot wide corridors.

And, of course, to nearly all who see her, she is in many ways the very symbol of Victoria.

*See Chapter 12 for further reference to this unique connection.

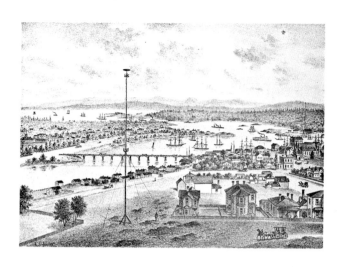

(Above) Old print of Victoria's harbor. The James Bay Bridge was replaced with a stone causeway and The Empress was built on reclaimed land to the left of the picture. (Below) The Birdcages, a popular name for the original legislative buildings, were replaced by the present buildings designed by Francis Rattenbury.

chapter 3

There Is No Such Place As Victoria

"To realize Victoria you must take all that the eye admires in Bournemouth, Torquay, the Isle of Wight, the happy valley at Hong Kong, the Doon, Sorrento and Camp's Bay - add reminiscences of the Thousand Islands and arrange the whole around the Bay of Naples with some Himalayas for the background."

Rudyard Kipling

To comprehend The Empress Hotel, to fully appreciate and savor it, it is necessary to know something of the city in which it stands. The two are inseparable.

What of Victoria?

Ethel Wilson, the grand lady of Canadian letters, gave us the best possible definition in one of her novels when she said that, of course, there is no such place as Victoria.

If this is true, then by the same token there is no such place as The Empress.

Yet they both seem to exist. We have thus far been introduced to the hotel. What, then, of the city?

It has been called a state of mind, and while this is not a unique attribute of Victoria, it is true of Victoria in a more exaggerated way than it is of many other cities. We commonly consider schizophrenia, a split personality, as being a double personality - one Jekyll and one Hyde. British Columbia's capital can only be described as existing in a state of polyphrenia because there are so many different versions of it held in so many different minds.

The mood of a particular visit filters out certain facets of the place, stressing this and eliminating that. The preconceptions of newcomers, the successes and desires of each of the 250,000 extreme individuals who inhabit the area, circumscribe and shape for each the city in which he lives. And this is particularly true of Victoria, since there are infinite permutations and combinations available in this balmy, rocky, historic, slumbering, vital, confusing, ludicrous, progressive patch of real estate at the southern tip of Vancouver Island.

Victoria is sometimes called a little bit of Olde England, a description as woefully incomplete of the city as it is of The Empress Hotel. Yet oddly enough, in peculiar ways, it has more truth in it today than it has had for several decades. This is so, at least if you consider England as it exists today. For as certainly as the modern era has created swinging London, so has today's youth created swinging Victoria.

In Victoria, it all started because of American pressure. The Hudson's Bay Company, chief architect of British Dominion in this part of the world, operated long on the coast out of Fort Vancouver, on the Columbia River, in what is now the state of Washington. As the Americans made it apparent to the great fur-traders that their time in that location was limited, they began to look around for another base.

As early as 1827 they had built a fort on the Fraser River on the mainland, Fort Langley. But its usefulness was limited and they wanted something more.

In 1842, James Douglas set out on the schooner Cadboro from Fort Vancouver to seek a new location on the southern tip of Vancouver Island. He examined what is known today as Sooke Harbor, Pedder Bay, the roadstead of Metchosin and the port of Esquimalt, finally deciding that the port of Camosack, or Camosun, should be established beside what we now know as the Inner Harbor.

Even so, he hedged. "The Situation is not faultless," he concluded his report, "or so completely suited to our Purposes as it might be; but I despair of any better being found on this Coast, as I am confident that there is no other Seaport North of the Columbia where so many Advantages will be found combined."

At any rate, in March of 1843 work began on Fort Victoria and southern Vancouver Island has never been the same since.

There was a flurry with the local Indians, but generally speaking things went as planned and in 1846, when the Oregon Boundary Treaty was finally signed and the British presence south of the 49th parallel ended, Fort Victoria became the chief western outpost of the Empire.

As time passed, James Douglas became Hudson's Bay boss in the region and, eventually, governor of the Crown Colony of Vancouver Island as well, a conflict of interests which agitated such local non-company residents as existed. Then in 1858, with the discovery of gold in the Fraser River, the world discovered Fort Victoria.

By the thousands, the fortune seekers came north. Victoria became a tent city teeming with milling mobs of miners from the played out California fields where the rush had started 10 years earlier.

James Douglas, perturbed lest this latest "invasion" would result in usurpation of the whole of the British mainland territory, as it had in Oregon, boldly asserted jurisdiction over the Mainland, too, though he had no legal right to do so, and began levying taxes and controlling the traffic to the gold fields. Eventually he was properly appointed governor of both colonies but in the process was forced at last to give up the Hudson's Bay Company post. Officialdom has not, it seems, changed much!

The miners brought with them a life and vitality that have remained just under the skin in the Victoria make-up. They also brought with them a Nova Scotian of a certain eccentricity and he has left a legacy that still persists in the Island city.

He called himself Amor de Cosmos, which he said meant "lover of the universe," though he was born William Smith. He set up a newspaper called the *British Colonist* which survives to this day as the *Times Colonist*. But where he was liberal to the point of being radical, engaging almost immediately in a

Victoria City Hall was saved from the wrecker's ball and dressed in its original finery. (Below) Bastion Square with Burnes House (L) and the old Court House (C). (B.C. Government Photo)

fight with the governor, the newspaper has switched sides of recent years.

Eight years after the gold rush the colonies on the Island and the Mainland were united into a single colony called British Columbia. And, low blow! The capital was moved to New Westminster, a blunder that the Island members of the legislature hastened to remedy with Victoria remaining the unchallenged capital of British Columbia since 1868.

This was the era when Canada was forming its confederation and the debate ranged fiercely on the Pacific Coast as to whether the colony should join Canada or the United States. A petition for annexation to the U.S. went out to the President from - that little bit of old England - Victoria and Vancouver Island.

The debate grew bitter, the chief opponent of confederation with Canada, on Vancouver Island at least, being Amor de Cosmos, by now editor of *The Standard*. However, Confederaton carried the day, B.C. joined the new dominion in 1871 and Victoria has been endeavoring to live down its past ever since.

By 1871, though, Fort Victoria as such had long gone. Victoria itself had municipal government from 1862, wrung out of the grudging Governor Douglas, and brick buildings were starting to rise. The first, known as Burnes House Hotel, later became a house of ill repute but now stands as a monument to urban renewal in beautiful Bastion Square.

All that was left of the fort, really, was Bastion Square plus a few names, notably Fort Street, a trail which wended its way to the fields outside the fort, or, if you prefer, from the fields into the fort. The site and area of Fort Victoria is now firmly indicated by a line of bricks embedded in the sidewalks on Government Street and around Bastion Square. Each brick bears the name of its donor.

The first legislative buildings, known as the Bird Cages because of their peculiar shape, had been built across the stinking swamp that was then the Inner Harbor, and a bridge run across to them. The road across the bridge extended on to the sea and became known as Government Street which was, we are told by the noted journalist and Victoria-phile Bruce Hutchison, the first street laid out in Canada west of the Rockies.

Years later, Hutchison explains, "the mud was drained, the basin filled and on the fill, with nothing but wooden piles to support its foundation, rose that elegant combination of French chateau and English manor house, The Empress Hotel."

But while other hotels were functioning in the immediate post-gold rush days, there was no Empress. There were, however, politicians, completing their debates with fist fights in the streets.

And in 1862 there arrived the good ship *Tynemouth*, a staunch iron screw steamer of 1,620 tons register and 600 horsepower. The *Tynemouth* carried 300 passengers but, said an artist and traveller named Frederick Whymper, "our most noticeable living freight was an invoice of sixty young ladies destined for the colonial and matrimonial market." They had been sent out by a home society under the watchful care of a clergyman and a matron; and they must have passed the dreariest three months of their existence on board, for they were isolated from the rest of the passengers and could only look on at the fun and amusements in which everyone else could take part.

The "invoice" of damsels was transferred at Esquimalt, even then a naval base, and brought round to Victoria proper.

Although the time and the place of disembarkation had been shrouded in mystery, as soon as it became known, a continuous stream of humanity set out toward the point indicated, which very shortly resulted in every available inch of ground from which a view could be obtained, being occupied by men of all ages, professions, trades, callings and stations in life, eagerly craning their necks for a sight of the unique, long-looked-for and much-discussed "cargo".

The "invoice" included a few mature women but most ranged from 12 to 18 years of age. Many soon went into service and about half married almost immediately. "A certain proportion went quickly to bad," reported Whymper, "and, from appearances, had been there before."

A second shipment of 36 damsels came out the next year with, apparently, somewhat more success.

Victoria by now was becoming a boisterous kind of place, a combined result of the American miners looking for gold and British sailors looking for fun. It seems hard to imagine, now, that in the final couple of decades of the last century Johnson Street was lined with saloons and bawdy houses.

Real estate and business boomed and bust and somehow the city gradually took shape. It was moulded, naturally, by its role as capital of B.C. and its social life centered around Government House and the Lieutenant-Governors. Furthermore, the ties of ritual and royalty were strengthened when officers and officials in the British forces and colonial services discovered the southern end of Vancouver Island.

These builders of Empire were a sad lot, really. They had been so long away from "home" enjoying, in many cases, freedom and privilege and stature they could not have aspired to in Mother England, that when it came time for them to retire they could not face the return. Climate had something to do with it too.

And so they came. They filled up Duncan, they spilled over into Saanich. And they became a large fact of life in Victoria.

They brought with them their titles and ranks, in some cases real wealth. They brought with them old school ties, and their eccentricities. With these, they set about to create in Victoria and its environs the kind of England their memory held for them. Thus it was that while there was much that was English in Victoria, it was never a bit of Olde England. It was colonial England done over in memory of an England that quite probably never really existed.

But they left their stamp, these stalwarts. Stout walking shoes, long scarves, "shops" instead of stores, and a strong demand for Peak Freans, Chivers, Wedgwood and Harris tweed.

They didn't mind that Victoria's streets were off the square; they fostered it. They fostered gardens, too, and started Victoria on its destiny as the "City of Gardens".

It was in the heyday of their time that The Empress was built, with the stone Causeway replacing the rickety bridge across to the James Bay district. The present parliament buildings, as the provincial legislature is grandiosely called, rose, too, forming the basis of the heart of Victoria - the Inner Harbor.

Bruce Hutchison wrote of this development thus: "For upward of 50 years Victoria has lavished its labor, money and invention on a precious area of some 20 acres. She has made it a stage set, a civic pantheon, a minor acropolis and altar of the Victorian spirit."

And for all the modern complaints that today's Causeway is, in the summer tourist season at least, a kind of gayway, a tasteless carnival of come-on to the supposedly moneyed visitor,

The Crystal Garden, across the street behind The Empress, was once the activity centre of Victoria. It is now fabulously renovated as a semi-tropical garden and aviary.

one can merely shrug and say that the beauty is there if you but look for it.

Perhaps the dominating feature of that precious 20 acres is still The Empress Hotel. The Empress stands back behind its lawns, aloof and unbending, untouched by the carnival over yonder, a proud symbol of Victoria from the day it was built.

When it was under construction, in 1907, there was a tiny house farther along Government Street, beyond the parliament buildings, in James Bay. In that house and later in another just off Government Street, lived an eccentric young woman who gradually became an eccentric old woman. She had a pet monkey, she kept boarders whom she seems to have hated, and she painted. Her name was Emily Carr. Her paintings, bold interpretations of the B.C. forests and Indian art, are national treasures. Her books are read and re-read. But she was scarcely acknowledged until it was almost too late.

Victoria is all these things out of the past, and therefore the Empress is part of them, too. But Victoria is many more things.

It is the twisting steep-steep one-way downhill run of Lotbiniere Avenue, sliding off Rockland Avenue next to Government House. It is hanging baskets of flowers from archaic cluster lamps. It is the new Royal British Columbia Museum and Archives. It is the ridiculous pomposity of the opening of the Provincial Legislature and the windswept yet tidy beauty of Beacon Hill Park.

It is love-ins staged by the hippy generation and it is, still, tea and crumpets at The Empress. It is the Garry oaks sloping before the wind all along the shore. It is the Maritime Museum in Bastion Square, it is the auction-room way of life. It is cars parked on Dallas Road so that the storm-tossed waves crash down upon the windshield. It is the famous painter of birds, Fenwick Lansdowne, it is modern industry, builders of the world's biggest offshore oildrilling rig, and it is the English sweet shops and the Royal London wax musuem.

It is the heart of an area that votes one way provincially and another federally. It is some of the worst drivers in B.C. and some of its best restaurants. It is a gaggle of churches, a splash of yellow broom.

It is the Chinese cemetery where tea is still put out by the graves. It is the Ross Bay Cemetery where lie Sir James Douglas who started it all, and Billy Barker who found the first gold at Barkerville and died a pauper.

It is a very old city, with much to show for its age. It is a city with youth in its heart, a city where the young are quick to assert themselves.

That is another reason why The Empress, with its extensive yet cautious and reserved renovations, fits so well.

Arthur Mayse, a noted editor and writer who now produces a weekly column for the *Times Colonist* newspaper once said of Victoria: "I've never seen a town which operated like this one on two main levels...the placid, contented, gardening elderly stratum overlying a reverse flow of quite vigorous younger people. There is a middle group that seems to be missing." But even the vigorous young grow older and the missing middle group are surfacing to the delight of developers eagerly erecting retirement homes and condominiums to house the influx of mature seekers of the somewhat laid back life style Vancouver Island offers.

There is still another big factor in Victoria's life...the University. The University of Victoria is one of the biggest things to have happened to the community in recent years. UVic, as it is called, is closely linked to the daily life of the area. Its influence spreads out through music, drama, painting, literature and in the bubble of life stirred by 13,000 students on their Gordon Head campus.

The British Columbia Ferry system, of course, has played a major role in rejuvenating the city, providing a direct, fast link with the provincial metropolis, that johnny-come-lately across the water called Vancouver.

But most of all, perhaps, Victoria is the unmatched rejuvenation of the downtown, where the good old has been treasured and refurbished, and complemented with the good new.

It all started with Centennial Square, in 1962. R.B. Wilson was mayor then and it was decided that something had to be done about the woefully inadequate old City Hall. Tear it down some said. But the mayor listened to architect Roderick Clack who said "No, paint it and add to it, it is a beautiful example of its era's architecture".

The mayor carried his council with him and today Victoria has an entire square with a magnificent fountain and a refurbished and beautiful civic theatre, as well as an historic City Hall of which it can be proud.

Of course, the City Hall has not always been a source of pride, even to Victoria's mayors. In fact, just four years after it was built, it went up for auction. Here is how the story has been told in the *Victoria Daily Times* under the heading "Auction the Mayor, Cried Crowd First Time City Hall Up for Sale".

"The Sheriff walked in, seized the corporation books, money, seal and assessment roll. Victoria city hall, only four years old, was on the market."

"It was December 19th, 1884. The city was twenty-two years old."

"Mayor J.W. Carey (after whom Carey Road is named) had refused to sign a cheque for $870.50. The bill had been submitted by the firm of Drake and Jackson. Mayor Carey would not accept responsibility for the bills of a previous administration."

"The sheriff took over. He placed a bailiff in charge of city hall and Mayor Carey placed a policeman in charge of the bailiff. The mayor complained he had not only been denied access to the hall, but he had also been assaulted."

"Council said the mayor should enter an action of $25,000 for damages and apply for an injunction to prevent the sheriff from selling the property."

On the 19th, the sheriff proceeded with his sale by auction and a large crowd gathered at the offices of auctioneer G. Byrne.

The *Victoria Daily Times* of December 19, 1884, reported one man was preparing to buy the city seal with the idea of selling it back at a profit when the council came to its senses.

"A prominent candidate for the mayoralty decided to purchase the mayor's chair and in it practice a graceful posture until elected, when he would bring both chair and posture to his inaugural meeting."

"Another citizen was eyeing the city safe."

"Sale was about to start when a group of thirteen staunch Victorians made their presence known."

"One, Joseph Spratt, climbed on a chair and beseeched all loyal citizens to abstain from bidding. He said he and his friends were prepared to put up the money to meet the judgment. There was loud applause and the sheriff accepted the offer. Mr. Spratt said the property would be returned to city hall and the corporation could go on corporating."

"Great cheering followed...among which could be heard cries of 'sell the council'...'put up the mayor'."

The Citizenry blamed Mayor Carey for disgracing the city and defeated him in the next election. R.P. Rithet won easily and his council repaid the 13 benefactors.

One of that group was the coal and railway baron, Member of Parliament for Victoria, Robert Dunsmuir.

This, of course, happened in other times. Pride in the civic square reactivated the whole downtown core, with businessmen quick to take advice on redecorating their buildings from the planners at City Hall and the city itself rescuing Bastion Square which had become a misery of a black-topped parking lot. Old buildings there were redone and the open square converted into a charming place for both citizens and visitors alike.

That makes it properly Victorian since Victoria is a place for people. For people to walk in, for people to move at their own pace in, for people to be themselves in. Dick Wilson, a former mayor and a third generation Victorian, said Victoria "offers an opportunity to be a little different".

This renovation of City Hall sparked newcomers to Victoria to continue the idea. Notable among them are Hans Hartwig and Sam Bawlf, who proved old buildings can be refurbished and internally modernized without destroying their aesthetic beauty, and still show a profit to the landlord.

Hartwig won awards with his Nootka Court (now Windsor Court) project and he has wrought wonders on Wharf Street. Bawlf, who resigned from Victoria city council when elected as Member of the Legislative Assembly for the city, has several projects under his belt. The Law Chambers Building in Bastion Square, the old Counting House at Broad and Broughton Streets, and his massive development creating Market Square in Old Town. More recently Michael Williams has converted many of the fine old, but derelict, buildings on lower Johnson and Pandora streets into attractive shops, hotels and restaurants.

Perhaps the most outstanding example of what can be done when parts of a city start to fade is, by Victoria standards, the massive Victoria Eaton Centre and Galleria covering two city blocks and replacing remnants of the famous Driard Hotel and other buildings of some heritage note, but also a number of small shops and offices of mixed distinction.

Being a little different has long been one of Victoria's famous characteristics, and no better example of it can be found than the intriguing tale of Louis the Lush. Louis was a South American macaw of indeterminate age, possibly a century old. He was the lifelong companion of a spinster named Victoria Jane Wilson and when she died she willed that her estate, before being divided between the Red Cross and Jubilee Hospital, should provide for Louis' care for life. So since 1949, Victoria Jane's faithful servant Wah Wong doled out Louis' daily diet of walnuts, almond, hard-boiled eggs and a spoonful of brandy.

The house has now been demolished and replaced with The Chateau Victoria Hotel, Victoria Jane's electric car has been sold and her 100 pairs of unworn gloves have gone to auction. Louis outlived his keeper, Wah Wong, which made the residual heirs restive. But, though shrouded with mystery, it is understood Louis has now been reunited with his mistress.

This is the kind of happening which was part of the old Victoria, and still flavors the world's picture of it. The robin in Christ Church Cathedral is another. While the magnificent church was being built, workmen found a robin had built its nest atop a pillar. Construction was continued around the little bird. One of the workmen marked the incident for all time by creating a nesting robin out of concrete. You can see it still, high up near the vaulted ceiling, to the right of the altar.

There are other shades of the past. There are Hatley Castle and Craigdarroch Castle, the former Dunsmuir estates. There is Trounce Alley, a heartwarming response of an independent-minded merchant named Trounce who in 1858 opened his own walk-through between Broad and Government streets when the city closed off View Street. Ever since, the charming by-way has been a popular shopping and coffee spot.

There is Craigflower School, built in 1885, and the oldest school building still standing in Western Canada. There is Point Ellice House where Scott, of Antarctica exploration fame, visited the beautiful Kathleen O'Reilly on frequent occasions. There are

Louis the Lush (above) is one bird that had few worries. His mistress provided handsomely for his retirement. (Bill Halkett Photo) The concrete robin in Victoria's Christ Church Cathedral (below) commemorates the compassion of a mason working on the church many years ago.

26

other assorted historic relics such as the fine display of Indian totem poles in Thunderbird Park. And Cadborosaurus the sea monster, any sightings of which will delight the Chamber of Commerce.

That august body of Victorian businessmen also spearheads Victorian Days each May long weekend. The locals are encouraged to deck themselves out in bustles or beards, and to try to recapture the old time atmosphere. Pennyfarthing bicycle races and rocking chair marathons are intermingled with North American institutions such as pancake breakfasts and wiener roasts. Despite the fact many Victorians are dressed for the period, many of them, it has been said, do not look very different all year round.

Victoria is all these things and a thousand more. And The Empress Hotel stands forever a part of them all, forever a part of the city.

Entertaining at teatime in the lobby, the Billy Tickle Trio (above) was almost an institution. At night they became the Bill Tickle Toe Tappers (below) and performed in the ballroom.

chapter 4

The Fiddler

"...a sane sort of music...at home in the opulence of The Empress."

Every time Billy Tickle drew a bow along his Italian-made violin in The Empress Hotel he had one thought: to honestly portray what the composer had in mind.

Named William Fletcher by parents in Cumberland, England, Tickle became plain Billy to the thousands who listened to his trio in the main lounge. The name stuck to him for the 32 1/2 years he played there.

He began his serenading, November 15, 1928, and as he used to say "A great many people put on a few pounds as they consumed the famous crumpets and honey" while he coaxed his instrument to speak the profound language of the masters. "But a great many people also gleaned tremendous enjoyment from my scratching on a piece of wood." Likewise the erudite Tickle. Music was his love since he could walk.

A man with less affection for a difficult art would never have acquired the inventory of scores that lined Tickle's basement shelves. All the great men were there, neatly stacked and tagged for immediate reference. Overtures, waltzes, operas, suites, sylvan dances, preludes...name it and Tickle could locate it with a flick of the forefinger.

The violin, cello and piano that comprised The Empress Hotel Trio performed for royalty more than once. Was Billy scared? Not on your life.

"There are two ways to play music," he would say. "Right and wrong. How this is done depends entirely on the player's ability, and I consider myself to have at least a little. Otherwise I would never have lasted."

Tickle's fame hinged around his fellow players. They always gave him their very best.

Undecided about the calibre of the day's music, Billy Tickle's habit was to play works of a "steady tempo." It was a "sane sort of music" intended to make guests feel relaxed and at home in the opulence of The Empress. How well he succeeded came from people's reactions.

A lady keeping time with her finger on the arm of a chair was a sure guarantee that he was on the right track. So was the smile and appreciative nod from the honeymoon couple tucked away in a little alcove by themselves.

Billy says it was heart-warming and encouraging. So, also, were the compliments paid him by notables of stage, film and radio fame. A thick album containing personally autographed photographs attests to these well-deserved kudos.

Tickle always catalogued in his mind the pieces popular with prominent guests, and, if he spotted them on return visits, he would greet them with their favorites. One traveller was regularly saluted with "Ah, Sweet Mystery of Life". A gay young Montreal lady once requested "I've Got A Loverly Bunch of Coconuts" and when it was played on each of her return visits, she fairly beamed.

Ann Carter, the actress, autographed a photo for Tickle and added "I love your music." When she returned 15 years later she wrote on the opposite side of the picture, "I still love your music."

National anthems caused Billy a lot of grief over the years. For one thing, he resolutely refused to play the national anthems of foreign countries. For another, he only once played "God Save the King" right through.

His refusal to play foreign anthems was tested one night by the cast of the movie "Commandos Strike at Dawn". The film was being shot in Victoria in the early days of the Second World War before the U.S. had entered the fracas, and a member of the cast requested "The Star Spangled Banner". When Billy refused, 14 people walked out.

But Billy got into the most trouble over "God Save the King". Many people considered him disloyal because he steadfastly declined to play more than the six bars of the shortened version. When pressed on the issue, he would pull from his wallet a newspaper clipping which stated the protocol - only the first six bars unless the sovereign was present. Billy played the entire Royal anthem for the first time in 1939 when King George VI and Queen Elizabeth were at the hotel.

The Saturday night dinner dances, when the augmented Billy Tickle Trio became Billy Tickle's Toe Tappers, was Victoria's "in" place for the "now" crowd of those days. But, in keeping with the times, many an anxious parent was known to ring Billy to enquire when and with whom their daughter had left the hotel. Naturally Billy dealt with the matter with true Empress diplomacy.

Tickle was always most at home during formal dinners. It provided the correct atmosphere for his melodic strains. He would refer to former days when dining was a religion, not a ritual, with everything in solid silver and each part of the meal served in a separate silver container.

Billy Tickle put on his last Empress performance May 15, 1960. He missed the life and the sound friendships he made over the years. Nevertheless, he accepted his retirement from the scene with a touch of plain philosophy knowing that sense is often a better bedfellow than sentiment.

"When you're well over 70 you run into trouble getting your fingers to behave as they should," is how he put it. "A stage, a phase, an era. It's as simple as that."

In 1975 Bill joined many of the great composers whose works he had enjoyed so much.

H.R.H. Prince of Wales autographed this photograph during his visit,
  September 1919.

chapter 5

A Princely Affair

"...Let's get on with the dance."

There have been many famous balls at The Empress Hotel over the years, but perhaps the most glittering was the gala held to honor the Prince of Wales, one of the chief organizers of which was Major George Nicholson whose books on west coast shipping are well known to British Columbians.

It was a fantastic night that 24th of September in 1919, and everything was laid on with precision by a committee appointed from the Navy and Army, the Veterans of France and the Great War Veterans' Association.

At precisely 5 p.m., The Empress, for the first time in its history, closed its doors to all but the registered guests who were given special identification cards.

CPR and Royal Canadian Mounted Police constables manned every entrance and 25 Mounties in dress uniform lined the driveway leading to the Belleville Street doors, reserved exclusively as the official entry for the Prince of Wales.

Soon the invitation holders began to appear, coming in through the basement door in the driveway off Humboldt Street. This entrance led into the billiard room which had been converted into a cloakroom, with 50 convalescent soldiers from the Esquimalt Military Hospital taking tickets and attending to other chores.

Promptly at 9 p.m. the bands struck up, Professor Lou Turner's 15-piece orchestra playing in the centre of the Palm

Court and alternating with the Great War Veterans' Association band under Bandmaster Rumsby located at the end of the ballroom. In the writing room, now the Bengal Room, Cecil Heaton's jazz orchestra compounded the rhythm by belting forth current hits of the day.

At 10 p.m. the Prince and two aides-de-camp arrived from Government House. Not on Belleville where the Mountie guard was waiting, but at the Humboldt Street basement entrance. There was momentary confusion before His Royal Highness was finally steered upstairs to be greeted by the reception committee and then escorted to his reserved suite on the first floor.

The full color of the ball was captured by Miss Ethel Bruce writing in the *Daily Colonist* of September 25, 1919:

"The scene at The Empress Hotel last night was one of unsurpassed brilliance. Arriving guests stepped from the spangled darkness of without into the fairy glamour of within, where the music and soft lights and the movements of hundreds of beautifully-dressed women and uniformed soldiers stirred the imagination happily to anticipate the coming of His Royal Highness the Prince of Wales, the guest of the evening."

"Passing through the north entrance the guests disposed of their wraps, the gentlemen in their dressing room in the basement; the ladies in well appointed rooms on the first floor. On the main floor, they joined the growing throng which scattered voluntarily through the three big rooms reserved for dance, the Foyer, the middle floor of which was completely cleared of its furnishings with the chairs and couches ranged around the walls for those who were not dancing, was little changed in other respects, although both here and in the palm-room enormous palms and other foliage plants formed an effective background for the party frocks worn by the ladies."

"The Centre dais in the Palm-room held Professor Turner's orchestra and at the north end was the buffet, with its big vases of chrysanthemums, at which cold drinks were served throughout the evening. On the door entering the long ballroom were the only flags displayed in the whole hall, these being two Union Jacks which formed the draperies across the entrance."

"The ballroom and writing-rooms were masterpieces of artistic decoration, representing the ingenuity of Mrs. Gertrude

Huntley Green and Mrs. Robert Baird, who were also responsible for the decorations in the grill-room."

"A feature of the decorations in the ballroom were huge baskets made by the convalescent soldiers at Esquimalt hospital. These were filled to overflowing with gladioli, Michaelmas daisies and trailing greenery. The light from a thousand lamps in the writing-room was softened with delicate rose-colored shades made by the wife of Lt. Col. J. C. Johnston, DSO."

"Most picturesque was the grill-room downstairs where ices and cold drinks were also served throughout the evening. The decorations here were Japanese, the cluster lights giving way to Japanese Lanterns, crimson, gold and green, which furnished a soft, yet gay light. The buffet was screened with autumn-tinted foliage and tapering baskets of chrysanthemums and cerise dahlias; crimson berries and gold and crimson maple leaves completed the effect of glorious coloring."

"The main dining room, where supper was served from ten o'clock on was arranged with a big horseshoe-shaped buffet in the middle, where a regiment of waiters supplied the wants of dancers admitted 300 at a time. Rose-colored chrysanthemums were used for the decorations. Salads, sandwiches, cake, jellies, ice cream and coffee were served; numerous small tables being provided for the guests' use in order to avoid congestion at the main buffet."

"His Royal Highness, showing no strain of the day's ceremonials, entered the foyer accompanied by Rear Admiral Sir Lionel Halsey, Lord Claude Hamilton, Commander North and other members of his entourage. He looked exceptionally boyish in his dress suit, which was relieved only by a row of decorations."

"After being greeted by Major-General R.G. Leckie, CMG, Brigadier R.P. Clark, DSO, Major F.B. Edwards and other members of the reception committee, the Prince made his way to the ballroom. He relaxed some of the formalities attendant to his princely rank and became just a boy bent on having a good time. As the band struck up a gay one-step, he swung out onto the floor with Mrs. Edwards as his partner, evidently enjoying the dance."

"At first the Prince was somewhat hampered by the throng of dancers who surrounded him, but as the evening wore on he was soon lost in the crowd and occasional glimpses of him during the whirl of the dance showed him in evident enjoyment."

"Later he danced with Lady Joan Mulholland, who had recently arrived from England and was a former Lady-in-Waiting to Princess Mary; Miss Peggy Hodgins, daughter of Lt. Col. and Mrs. A.E. Hodgins, Miss Gwyneth McPhillips, Mrs. George Nicholson, Miss Eleanor Monteith, Miss Peggy McBride, Miss Brownie Bodwell and Mrs. A.E. Jukes. His Royal Highness went to supper about midnight, taking in Mrs. Nicholson, his partner just previous."

The financial side of the Ball was also a success. Over a thousand tickets sold at $5 each, for both men and women. Only two complimentary tickets were issued and those to the women's page editors of the *Colonist* and *Times* respectively. Lieutenant-Governor Sir Frank Barnard purchased 15 tickets for himself and the Government House party. Cabinet ministers purchased theirs also. So did every member of the committee.

Net returns were $926.65, for which amount a cheque was handed over to the Widows and Orphans of Ex-Service Men's fund.

As His Royal Highness had been closely associated with and actually served for a time on the staff of the Canadian Corps in France, a large block of tickets was set aside exclusively for returned men and their families. Informal was not only welcomed, but encouraged; however, formal dress was worn by most of those present.

With each ticket went a souvenir invitation beautifully gilt embossed with the recipient's name individually hand-engraved.

The hundred or so regular guests of The Empress would have been free to mingle at the ball but every one of them bought a ticket, largely through the activities of Herb Wilson, The Empress' manager at the time.

All in all it was quite a glittering affair, not without humor and odd consequences since the following morning one of the revelers, a member of the legislative assembly, awoke to find himself stretched out in a bathtub in the company of a live octopus.

And there is also the report that at midnight, when the aides thought it was time for the heir to the throne to go home, the strains of "God Save the King" sounded throughout the halls. The Prince of Wales thought differently. As the majestic music ended, the Royal voice was heard to say: "Now we've put father to bed, let's get on with the dance."

chapter 6

The Walker

"Not a hotel, The Empress is a way of life."

For 47 years Howard Hemming's job kept him within nine acres yet he walked hundreds of miles doing it.

He was Chief Engineer at The Empress until his retirement in July 1967.

A trim, fast talking, fast thinking, and for that matter fast walking man, Hemming remembers the area before the hotel was even built.

"I was four years old," he says "The place The Empress stands on now was a kind of slough with an old wooden bridge across where the causeway now stretches."

After the turn of the century, in 1904, the Canadian Pacific Railway Company and the City of Victoria had signed a joint contract to fill in the mud flats east of the old wooden bridge joining James Bay to the city proper. Using cut stone from Haddington Island, the causeway came first and behind it the slough was filled in with anything dumpable plus sludge dredged from the harbor. Some people still living in Victoria claim they can well remember the appalling aroma which hung over the city at the time with the populace then referring to the site as the city dump.

It was in those days that a local garbage collector made a killing. Bill Miner was paid to clean a section of street by the local shopkeepers. This he did, loading his barrow and trundling it off until nightfall when he would cunningly dump it in another street. The following day he would approach the second group of shopkeepers suggesting their street was a mess and undertake to clean things up for a consideration. Such an arrangement would probably not have continued for long in any case. It did come to a halt, though, when the demand for fill for The Empress site afforded Bill a more accessible dump without the trouble of clearing up the same garbage two or three times in succession. Hemming recalls that the job of reclaiming the flats and building the hotel took from 1904 to January 1908.

"I have a vague memory of the work going on although at my age then I was asleep a lot of the time. Even in those days they were laboring around the clock under what passed for floodlights. Bales and bales of straw were dumped into the morass to give some sort of footing for the workmen, while pile drivers thumped day and night driving 125-foot piles as close together as possible until they reached bedrock.

"They evidently succeeded because those same piles can be seen to this day in certain places way below the hotel where we have made special inspection cut-aways. They are as good as the day they were driven, pickled I guess in the brine and sludge. And solid! Why the old place barely quivered during an earthquake in 1963. A joint slightly pulled on the main staircase. A crack of plaster here and there, and that was it. As I say, solid as a rock.

Understandably so. The walls of the ground floor are 30 inches thick. In engineering language, enough to support a small city. From then on, it's brick atop brick...thousands of them...right up to the tenth floor.

Architecturally, there is no building like The Empress in all Canada. There are those who say it would be impossible to duplicate it these days. Hemming insists it confutes all modern techniques and approaches. The planners evidently drew a sketch of what they wanted, and started from that.

The apex of the original building demonstrates how the construction was done. Great wooden beams, criss-crossed and angled to fit, give the interior a fortress-like appearance. How did they get these huge pieces up to that height? Hemming is unable to explain though he has to suppose they were hauled skywards by muscle power via block and tackle. The tenth floor roof is covered with slates approximately 10 by 18 inches and, every now and then, workmen have to slide along the almost vertical roofs to replace the slates. "One thing about it," says Hemming, "is the superb view the men get of Victoria."

After all the time he spent tending the miles and miles of pipes and electrical wiring, Hemming came to know every nook and cranny within the baronial walls of The Empress. A master key gave him entry to each room. He learned the various ways to reach the upper storeys, one of them by concrete steps that, flight after flight, seem to go on towards the clouds. He has walked them all...thousands of times.

The sixth floor was the maids' original quarters. Windows several feet above the floor are said to have kept the damsels from waving to their beaux along Government Street, but they also gave a more satisfying appearance to the building from the outside.

To enter any one of these rooms is to enter a thousand like them in the old estates of the British Isles and Europe. Something about them speaks of history, wars at sea, the heyday of an Empire, flowing gowns, bemedalled tunics, proclamations, great crocks of mead, goblets of wine and music drifting out to balconies where romance was whispered.

As for balconies, The Empress has many. One in front is where kings and queens and princes and princesses have acknowledged the cheers and plaudits of the crowds. Above it, imperious and enriching, flutters the flag of British Columbia.

Though alike architecturally, each 12-foot-wide corridor clearly evinces its own distinctive atmosphere. This is where long-time residents walked and talked and remembered. It is where, in the evening light, veterans recall hand-to-hand battles abroad and terrific sense of duty and obligation to country that history might well never again experience. It is where love in the autumn of life still glows with very special tenderness, frequently only by a memory. And it is where differences are discussed, be they religion, politics, the stock exchange or atomic bombs.

Newcomers to The Empress are shown to their quarters along these carpeted pathways. Immediately there falls upon them a hush that, if they cared to talk about it, they would possibly describe as reverence. So far, no one has been quite able to explain the reason. But just as many have expressed impatience when they tried to retrace their steps. One guest suggested management should issue a set of blueprints so that people wouldn't get lost, or else supply electric golf carts to make it easier to get around.

Home for 20 years and more to people from many parts of the world, certain rooms in The Empress were actually suites, fireplaces and connecting doors included. Seagulls knew the windows well; they belonged to those guests who persisted in feeding the birds despite the efforts of management to discourage the practice. Also relying on hand-outs, pigeons shelter in the stonework niches and produce their broods.

Huge wooden pillars grace foyers and support staircases, the work entailed both immense and intricate. Possibly, for instance, the spacious dining room has few counterparts anywhere. Likewise the panelled banquet rooms in the basement, scenes of many a gathering, and given royal titles to further enhance their dignity. The main entrance hall is where people on their first visit stop for a moment and hold their breath.

Hence, from a puddle in the ground, The Empress has risen up her regal head by a system of architecture that would send the modern planner off one of the several parapets if he had to tolerate it today. Alone and extremely singular, she has managed to defy expert and extremist and, by so doing, has brought charm, warmth and happy memories to those who have rested and sheltered within her unconventional confines.

"Not a hotel," Howard Hemming sums it, "The Empress is a way of life. In every one of her moods, winter and summer, and believe me I've found her fractious and temperamental at times, I still have nothing but good to say of her. With all these new improvements, furnishings and modern equipment she's good for many years and more. Long may she reign over us and I'll still be walking round in the evenings just to gaze at the old lady!"

Others have followed Howard Hemming's footsteps as Chief Engineers or Superintendents of Maintenance, absorbing additional responsibilities refurbishing and up-dating the hotel's facilities. Each have displayed affection and understanding of the foibles of a grand lady.

"Reginald spoke to them yesterday and, I thought at the time, made our feelings on the matter quite clear..."

Norris cartoon reprinted from *Vancouver Sun* by permission of Stuart Keate, Publisher

43

Shirley Temple (upper left) and John Wayne (upper right) are two of the many celebrities that have passed through The Empress over the years. (Bottom) A quiet moment in the lobby in the 1970's.

chapter 7

Once Upon A Time...

"...there is always just Victoria with its clustered lampposts festooned with flowers, its people worth taking time to talk to, its life worth taking time to live."

National Geographic

The lobby of The Empress is a very special place. It is undeniably different.

Many so-called grand hotels have lobbies with ceilings just as high. Some even have lobbies with as much sheer space. But there is an unhappy tendancy about such hotel lobbies to become cold and unfriendly. Sounds echo. There are few, if any, corners to hide in. Traffic tends to be heavy, with arriving and departing guests and their luggage lending a sense of urgency.

Not so the lobby at The Empress. In the fifties one eastern Canadian writer described the hotel's decor, by which he obviously was thinking chiefly of the lobby, as "early parsonage parlor, with most of its furnishings a bit too young to be called antique and too old to be called comfortable".

On the other hand, a writer for a Seattle newspaper described entering The Empress lobby as a rare emotional experience somewhat akin to visiting Westminster Abbey. This begins to get the idea but it also overstates to the point of obscuring it.

The main impression given by the lobby of The Empress is its tone. It is at once formal and friendly, congenial yet subdued, except at the height of the summer season.

True, when you enter The Empress you tend to lower your voice. You could shout if you wanted to and probably attract less attention than in most hotels. But you don't. You just don't. You look around at the plants and the people, and there are fewer of both ensconced there than tradition would have it, and you decide that it would simply not do to bellow across the room.

The lobby of The Empress Hotel is good manners. But then you could say that has been the motto of the hotel since its inception. The Empress has a long tradition of being discreet, of seldom questioning and then only in the quietest way, and of protecting the privacy of its guests.

Over the years, The Empress has been host to kings and queens, to presidents, generals, socialites and social climbers, movie stars and sports celebrities. Among its millions of guests it has also, of course, included a very great many plain ordinary people.

Perhaps its most famous guests, certainly its most storied ones, were the Empress dowagers, the elderly ladies who lived out the last years of their lives in The Empress' rooms and, naturally, in the lobby.

In the earliest years these permanent residents were wealthy Edwardian widows, accustomed to the best and insisting on it to the end.

Many were the widows of self-made millionaires or retired Colonial officials and they would appear for dinner each evening in long flowing dresses with lace mittens covering the fingers so carefully curled around their lorgnettes. Always accenting their costumes were expensive necklaces and brooches and exaggerated make-up complemented by the fragrance of good, and expensive perfume.

The ladies took it as a right that the maitre d'hotel would personally escort them to their seats, the same seat at the same table every night. Each had her special seat, too, in the rotunda, where she would retire after dinner to listen to the mellow sounds of Billy Tickle's strings until that precise moment when it was time for cards.

Three tables were set for the group next to the conservatory, and they would play, mostly in silence, for three hours each evening. Transient guests would be entranced by this performance and gradually edge closer until the kibitzing drew such icy stares from the players it caused all but the hardiest onlooker to withdraw in confusion.

If stares alone proved not enough, or if some outlanders actually desecrated the evening by sitting at the ladies' card tables, a few low-keyed but withering words would send the interlopers packing.

The era of these grandes dames came to an end with the great depression of 1929. True, the ladies themselves stayed on in many cases and they carried off their new-found poverty with great style, but behind the scenes things were vastly different.

The Empress itself was hard hit by the depression, finding that it had more staff than guests - a situation not conducive to black ink in the ledgers. The management did what it could. A special low rate was introduced for resident guests taking rooms on the top floor. This was indeed a boon to the newly impoverished widows who could live in The Empress and use its stately public rooms as their living room.

At first, the new Empress dowagers ate in the dining room but, one by one, they disappeared. It was gradually discovered they were converting their upstairs quarters into housekeeping rooms. Hotplates were surreptitiously smuggled in and shelves improvised for storing groceries.

The Empress management sighed and in all but the most flagrant cases, said nothing. Soon, though, the stories started winding their way down the side corridors and staircases.

There was the small but charming and fashionably dressed woman who ventured down for tea one afternoon and when the waitress approached ordered merely a pot of hot water. Although somewhat taken aback, the waitress brought the water and a cup and then watched in fascination while her customer opened her purse, pulled out a tea-bag and brewed up. Then she drank two cups of tea in full company of the other Empress guests. This performance continued for many months, much to the admiration of the staff who considered its role in the proceedings all a part of The Empress' service.

Another of these $1 a day guests appeared for breakfast every second day. When her meal arrived she carefully divided it, eating half and tucking the rest in her purse to provide for tomorrow.

There is also a tale told of the elderly lady who demanded special attention and the best cuts of beef and when it wasn't forthcoming would pitch the offending roast clear across the dining room.

One of the resident dowagers had her bath covered with boards to hold all the jam, jelly and honey given to her by doting relatives. These, and the potted plants she had ranged in solid phalanx about her room, made it quite impossible to clean the windows on the inside.

Another guest is said to have made strawberry jam on her hotplate. A third had to be asked, most gently, to refrain from cooking liver and onions in her room, and a fourth not to pickle onions.

Perhaps one of the most celebrated of the Empress dowagers was a titled lady (courtesy withholds her name). Always the most elegantly attired among the permanent guests, generally in flowing gowns but with one fashionable inconsistency of the times. Day in and day out she wore a somewhat aged pair of canvas tennis shoes. Little did she know her fad was the forerunner of a worldwide love affair with Nikes, Reeboks and L.A. Gear.

The old reading room, now the Bengal Room, was a favorite spot for some of Victoria's citizenry to rest and spend the time of day and at least two regulars developed the habit of bringing in their lunches. The Empress looked the other way until they spilled sardine oil on the carpet. Then it was tactfully suggested they might care to lunch elsewhere.

Nor have bird lovers missed out on the action over the years. Seagulls from the Inner Harbor were inevitably befriended by numbers of the regular guests who left tidbits on the window ledges for the winged foragers. On a certain memorable night, a guest who had pampered the birds returned from an evening visit to her nephew with a plucked chicken and placed it on the window ledge to keep it cool until she cooked it on her hotplate next day. A visiting seagull with a finders-keepers complex promptly tried to help himself but the chicken proving too heavy merely tumbled over the edge of the sill into the shrubbery far below. Undaunted, the chicken's owner flounced forth to retrieve her game and when a surprised gardener who spotted her peering in among the bushes asked what was up, the answer must also have been surprising coming even from an Empress dowager - "My good man," she replied haughtily, "I'm down here looking for my chicken."

Also popular in Empress annals are tales of guests who came for two weeks and stayed 20 years, of others who brought in their own furniture. Of members of a family related to the Pierpont Morgans. They arrived every spring with their own valet, maid and doctor. In fact, the celebrated visitors set up their headquarters within the boundaries of the hotel. Prominent in the American edition of *Who's Who*, their winter residence was given as New York but their summer home was listed as The Empress, Victoria.

Then there was the "regular" of sartorial splendor from San Francisco who would never touch money. If it was necessary for him to remove so much as a coin from his pocket, he would carefully don a spotless pair of yellow kid gloves before deigning to touch the lucre.

Another lady visitor from the far east, came to Victoria aboard a famous Empress steamer, accompanied by no less than 13 large trunks one of which contained a series of wooden blocks. Before this guest would retire the hotel staff had to arrange her bed at a certain angle facing the east with the aid of the blocks, and, since she only stayed a day or so, it was hoped she found service to equal that of The Empress at other hotels she chose to check into during her subsequent tour across the continent.

The Empress has played host to Raymond Collishaw, the Canadian fighter ace who destroyed 60 enemy planes during the First World War, and to Wing Commander Guy Gibson who, as leader of the famous "dam busters" won the Victoria Cross during the Second World War.

It sheltered Charles and Ann Lindbergh on their way home from China to attend the funeral of Ann Lindbergh's father, Dwight Morrow.

Other famous guests have been legion, from Rudyard Kipling to Shirley Temple, from the late Jack Benny and Spencer Tracy, Bing Crosby and John Wayne to Bob Hope and Rita Hayworth, from Van Cliburn, Rostropovich and Philippe Entremont to Bobby Riggs, from Haile Selassie to the Los Angeles Kings.

H.R.H. Prince of Wales and his brother the Duke of Kent are accompanied by B.C. Lieutenant-Governor Bruce (L) and B.C. Premier McLean (C). (Below) President Roosevelt with B.C. Lieutenant-Governor Eric W. Hamber (R) on their way to The Empress, September 30, 1937.

During the day when he was in a political wilderness between world wars, Winston Churchill, with his son Randolph, visited Victoria. It was during prohibition and the great man was speaking at a large dinner in the hotel's main ballroom. In deference to the quaint liquor laws then in effect, Churchill was served his whiskey in a silver teapot, the water neatly concealed in a matching cream jug.

Another renowned Briton to sign the register was Lord Jellicoe, fresh from his celebrated First World War victory over the German fleet.

Royalty has called here as well with, of course, several visits from members of the British Royal family. On the occasion of a state luncheon given in honor of King George VI and Queen Elizabeth, the dignity of the affair was shattered by an explosion. Mounties and secret service men dashed to the scene only to find a somewhat chagrined press photographer - plus the shattered remains of an exploded flash bulb.

Perhaps the royal visitors who caused the most curiosity were King Prajadhipok and Queen Rambai Barni of Siam who chose to visit in the between-wars period with a retinue of 56 attendants and 556 pieces of baggage. A complete floor was reserved for the party and special section of the kitchen set aside in which Siamese cooks prepared special foods for the visiting monarchs.

The Siamese royal couple had, on their way across the Pacific, participated in the record-breaking run of the CPR's Pacific flagship, *Empress of Japan*. The first time the eight-day mark had been broken, the sea-going *Empress* covered the 4,260 miles from Yokohama to Victoria in seven days, 20 hours and 16 minutes, carrying one of the richest cargos ever to cross that particular ocean - $10,000,000 worth of raw silk from Japan. The sleek *Empress* made the crossing at full throttle in order to get the prized cargo trans-shipped to New York by rail in championship time. Eventually, this silk trade became an important part of the great CPR Pacific fleet and whenever such a cargo reached dockside, it would be expressly cleared and sent over to the mainland that same night to catch the special train east.

In the history of The Empress Hotel, American officialdom has also cut quite a swath. On one occasion, Franklin D. Roosevelt headed a meeting between Canadian and American

Their Majesties King George VI and Queen Elizabeth on the steps of the hotel during their visit, May 1939.

authorities dealing with Pacific Coast Defences. Accompanied by Mayor Fiorello LaGuardia of New York City, then American chairman of the Joint Defence Board, the discussions resulted in an extensive system of defences on the southern tip of the Strait of Juan de Fuca installed and ready before Pearl Harbor to protect Victoria, Vancouver, Seattle, Tacoma, Olympia and the entire Puget Sound/Strait of Georgia region from conventional sea-borne attack.

Probably, though, the greatest array of American politicians to assemble outside their own country met in The Empress under the wing of John Knox Garner, Vice-President of the United States. A boatload of American legislators, including the Speakers of both the House of Representatives and the Senate were guests at a dinner tendered by the government of British Columbia. The oratory lasted long into the night.

Conventions, of course, play a big part in the continuing life of the grand old hotel.

Shriners have turned the afternoon tea hour topsy turvy barging into the lobby by the hundreds, led by their fifes and drums. The lobby is also a favorite gathering spot, believe it or not, for loggers' conventions whose activities hardly match up to the Empress myth.

In 1941, the PEO Sisterhood held its biennial supreme convention outside the United States for the first time in the organization's history - at The Empress of course. A thousand women were packed into the hotel and to accommodate them several of the public rooms were turned into dormitories and furnished with rows of beds, wash basins and chairs.

The PEO's grand evening event took place in the Crystal Ballroom where a large pool, complete with waterfall, was installed and Indian canoes were paddled by conventioneers singing such appropriate songs as "By the Waters of Minnetonka". When it came time for the speeches, however, the waterfall drowned out the orations until the hotel plumber was called onto the scene to make the proper adjustments.

Hotel officials say, with some apparent surprise, despite the fact so many guests were so closely packed in such confined spaces there were fewer complaints than normally arise even out of much smaller conventions. And glass breakage was nil.

*State luncheon October 22, 1951. B.C. Lieutenant-Governor Clarence
Wallace with H.R.H. Princess Elizabeth who is receiving a gift from B.C.
Premier Byron Johnson. (R) H.R.H. The Duke of Edinburgh looks on.
(Below) H.M. Queen Elizabeth leaves the hotel, May 14, 1971 after an
official visit.*

Nor had the world of sports failed to make a play at the hotel. Just once in its history Victoria boasted a hockey team that won the Stanley Cup and, fittingly enough, The Empress figured in the story.

It was 1925 when the Flying Frenchmen from Montreal arrived. The Canadiens filed into the hotel lobby behind their finely turned out manager Leo Dandurand replete with spats, cream suede gloves, a homburg hat and a gold-headed cane. Behind him came such famous players as Howie Morenz, Auriel Joliat and Georges Vezina, after whom the Vezina trophy for goalkeeping honors is named. The team brought with them a great reputation and the full confidence of eastern Canada they would take home the Stanley Cup. But when they left for home ten days later they had been beaten three out of four games by the Victoria Cougars.

Canadian football's annual Grey Cup classic has likewise spilled over into the ample arms of the grand old lady. Vancouver's Empire Stadium was the locale of the exciting game between the Edmonton Eskimos and Montreal Alouettes, yet the Eskimos decided to train in Victoria and the Edmontonians added a distinctly new tone to The Empress lobby as twice each day they walked across the heavy carpets in their stockinged feet, sitting on the front steps to put on their cleated boots before setting out for practice.

The football players proved a great hit with The Empress dowagers, too, since many of the guests had removed themselves from the icy prairies to live in the balmier Island climate. Naturally the dowagers wanted to wish the prairie team well and so it was that such giants of the gridiron as Normie Kwong, "The China Clipper", 220-pound John Bright and Jackie "Mr. Twinkletoes" Parker were found taking tea in The Empress lobby with their somewhat elderly but still avid fans.

Not all The Empress' connections with great sporting events have taken place in the mundane way of merely providing rooms for the participants. The Empress (and probably no other hotel can make this statement) has itself been the scene of a golf championship final. That happened when the CPR, in its largely successful efforts to promote the beauties of Victoria's temperate winter climate, yearly staged a midwinter golf tournament attracting players from the U.S. and the Canadian prairies. One year, as years will do, the snow came, blanketing the Colwood course on the day of the final.

Hurriedly, the spacious Georgian Room at The Empress was converted into a miniature nine-hole course with rugs covering the entire floor ruffled in places to provide the "rough". The finalists were allowed to use only putters - and the match was completed.

The Empress bridal suite was the most occupied guest room in the hotel. It appeared to be permanently under reservation and frankly the hotel could almost do with half a dozen bridal suites to cope with the steady demand. It is not unusual for The Empress to have 10 or 12 honeymoon couples under its roof at the same time. This shocking situation has now been addressed with a romantic attic with a number of exquisite honeymoon suites accessible only by a staircase above the sixth floor.

Since the hotel opened, probably more than 100,000 couples have embarked on the sea of matrimony with a view of Victoria's Inner Harbor from their room. And although the hotel staff respects the privacy of guests it is admitted notables such as former president Richard Nixon and his bride spent the first few days of their married life in the hotel.

Nor do British Columbians forget when Government House, the official residence of British Columbia's Lieutenant-Governors, burned down in 1957. It seemed only logical at the time to transfer the whole vice-regal scene to The Empress. A more fitting choice could not have been made. As the Queen's representative, His Honor Frank M. Ross with Mrs. Ross operated out of the hotel for two years, during which the province celebrated the first of a rash of centennials highlighted by a visit from Princess Margaret accompanied by a floor-filling retinue of aides, ladies-in-waiting and attendant dignitaries.

Time and tide have perforce changed certain nostalgic pictures at The Empress. Many more will change. Billy Tickle has gone. Today, $1 a day rooms cost about $5 an hour, afternoon tea, which used to crumpet in at 35 cents has risen proportionately. The reading room has become the Bengal Room and the writing room is now a commercial gallery of Native art, with very little reading or writing done in either. Car parking is neatly tucked away beneath the adjoining Conference Centre.

For many years commercial travelers displayed their wares in a number of spacious suites on the ground floor of the Towers Wing, on Humboldt Street. The suites in this area contain offices, shops, and the "Miniature World" exhibition.

Few regulars frequent the lobby now - real regulars, that is, people who would develop a sense of family involvement such as the man who occupied the same chair beside the grandfather's clock in the lobby for almost 15 years. When he died, the hotel placed a wreath in the chair for a week and none of his acquaintances ever sat in it again.

For many years a number of portraits of the wives of Canada's Governors General hung on the panelled walls of the dining room. When asked by visitors who the ladies were, many a waitress twitted the diners the portraits were those of past manager's wives or retired waitresses. The portraits now have been tastefully distributed throughout the guest room corridors with an informative plaque beside them.

Also continuing to claim their just share of attention are The Empress gardens which have long been a famous Victoria attraction, their greenhouses bulging with blooms of every description grown specially to enhance the rooms and tables of the hotel. In 1989 the gardens were greatly expanded and enhanced. A fitting tribute to Victoria the city of gardens.

When occasion has demanded The Empress has dealt diplomatically with strikers and streakers - the latter had the good taste to wear neckties through the lobby. Even a gunman made an attempted hold-up. Not at the front office in the reception area, but more discreetly in the Garden Cafe. The cashier informed him this sort of thing was just not done in The Empress. Somewhat shaken, the fellow fired a shot into the ceiling and left lootless.

For many years there was a pretty rock garden and pond in the corner of the grounds among the trees near the corner of Humboldt and Government streets. Each spring a special family of ducks nested nearby, hatching out its brood and spending the summer amid the plush surroundings. Every morning, when the coffee shop opened at 7.30, the ducks presented themselves for breakfast and then walked off under the bridge and into the gardens at the back of the hotel. Unbelievable though it may seem, these particular ducks have been known to escort their

(Above) The Royal yacht Britannia *was berthed in front of The Empress in May 1971. (Below) H.R.H. Princess Margaret is welcomed to The Empress by B.C. Lieutenant-Governor Frank Ross in 1958.*

young across Belleville Street and the two blocks up the hill on Douglas Street to Beacon Hill Park, there to visit with relatives and return in the evening to their own pond. New construction has unfortunately forced the ducks to move in permanently with their relatives.

All of which proves neither flesh nor fowl fails to find the right way to reach this stateliest of historic inns.

And there are undoubtedly many aficionados still around ready to agree with the gentleman who raged with indignation when the big Empress sign was first raised above the front entrance.

"Anyone," he spluttered, "who doesn't know this is The Empress shouldn't be staying here!"

The conservatory was built in 1929 and became a focal point for photographers.

chapter 8

Behind The Desk

From the time The Empress opened its doors in 1908 there have been numerous colorful personalities closely connected with its operation.

Recorded elsewhere in the book are the names of Captain J.W. Troup and George Henry Barnard and the leading part they played in establishing the need for, and in the ultimate construction of the hotel. At that time the president of the Canadian Pacific Railway, Sir Thomas Shaughnessy, had delegated the company's interests and responsibilities to Hayter Reed, superintendent for Canadian Pacific Hotels, and to George Ham, a company executive from Montreal.

It was at the opening ceremonies, January 20th, 1908, when these two gentlemen really came into their own. The official ceremonies involved a luncheon for some 50 representatives of the press from Canada and the western United States. Hayter Reed spoke at considerable length in praise of his boss' foresight in providing this magnificent facility and not without justifiable pride did he pay glowing tribute to his wife who had planned the interior decorations and furnishings. Mrs. Hayter Reed had been capably assisted by her sister, Mrs. Stewart Gordon, and to keep the whole operation under neat, cosy, control, Mrs. Stewart Gordon's husband was appointed hotel manager. At the same gathering, Hayter Reed introduced several personalities of the day including Captain Clive Phillips-Wooley whom he described as the poet laureate of British Columbia. The gallant captain quickly disclaimed the title but according to the local *Colonist* newspaper's account the following day, proceeded to wax somewhat lyrical with the following phrases.

"This is a wedding feast. Victoria has long been waiting for its Prince Charming. Victoria has been sleeping for half a century. She stirred slightly when Douglas came and Davie half wakened her. But now the CPR has finally roused her under Sir Thomas Shaughnessy. Victoria waited for the kiss of love and now comes into her own."

Pretty heady stuff for an old soldier, though some people suggest the kiss did not linger long before Victoria turned over and went back to sleep for 50 years. Then in 1962 British Columbia's Premier W.A.C. Bennett planted a stirring smacker on the sleeping beauty with a shiny new fleet of B.C. Ferries. Incidentally, the captain later became a Knight, for services not divulged in available records. Could it have been for "poetry"?

The visiting guest who made the official vote of thanks at the luncheon was the editor of the *Seattle Marine and Railway News*, Percy Parkinson. The final personality to round out the ceremonies was George Ham who lived right up to his name with an address which had the well-lubricated guests rolling in the aisles and again it was for the *Victoria Colonist* of January 21st of that year to spotlight the epoch-making event with this quote.

"It was not until the tolling of the bells announced the hour of midnight that the gathering broke up and all knew that the formal opening of The Empress Hotel upon the North American continent was a thing of the past. The Empress was opened."

From thereon the hotel settled into a busy routine under a series of managers starting with Steward Gordon, followed in fairly close succession by Colonel B.M. Humble, and Messrs. H. Jackson, A. Benaglia, T. Coles, W. Windross, B.F. Quail and J.O. Evans. Colonel Humble returned for another stint in 1919. H.J. Wilson took over in 1921 and in June 1931, Kirk Hodges moved from his position as assistant manager to the top post which he held for a record 21 years. With his charming wife, Hodges set a pattern of high social activities in and around The Empress. Introducing such innovations as the famous "Empress Golf Week", he kept the standard of guests top drawer. "We had very little trouble with undesirables," Hodges explained, but admitted even with a high class clientele the hotel did lose its share of silver and towels.

In 1953 Thomas E. Chester, accompanied by his wife Helen and two daughters, Doris and Phyllis, arrived to take over the helm of a hotel in which he had once worked as accountant. Tom Chester had already served the Canadian Pacific Hotels system in various capacities and could be truly described as a dyed-in-the-wool hotelier since his birth at the family-owned Cross Keyes Inn in Western Rhyn, Shropshire, England. Unfortunately, age and health prevented Chester from remaining at his post for more than two years and in 1955 Cyril Chapman was appointed to the top job enabling Chester to retire. Chapman had worked his way up through the CPR hotel ranks in Toronto, Regina, Winnipeg and Lake Louise. For 20 years he managed the celebrated Seignory Club at Montebello, Quebec, and his appointment to The Empress instigated many new trends during his eight year tenure. He says his job at The Empress was to "flutter her skirts and show a bit of shapely leg," and some of his innovations horrified Victorians such as the large plastic sign across the Government Street entrance. In the early 60's, Chapman also opened a large wing of the hotel as a Motor Lodge where guests carried their own luggage and enjoyed other economies in the service. For a time the Motor Lodge served its purpose until new facilities were built in the surrounding area by enterprising motel operators. With their advent, the Motor Lodge closed down.

In 1963 at the suggestion of his doctor, Cyril Chapman repaired to the mainland and the more sedate management of the Vancouver Club and the manager's desk at The Empress was taken over by another CPR man with many years service under his slim belt.

Leslie C. Parkinson was noted for his swinging style of operation. Born in Bristol, England, in a year not divulged, Leslie Parkinson came to Canada as an infant. In 1929 he joined the Royal York Hotel in Toronto.

Parkinson continued the Chapman pattern of raising the hemline and diagnosing the deficiencies of the old lady of Government Street. His wartime experiences must have created considerable stamina for Parkinson faced the firing line of irrate Victorians and visitors, civic officials and company directors with equanimity over the dozens of schemes and plans to convert nine acres of prime downtown land into something more profitable than a running love affair with an ivy-clad tradition.

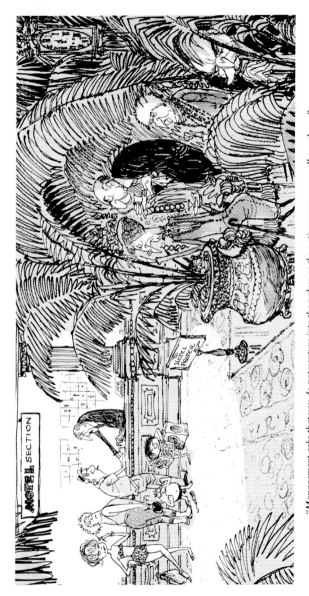

"*Management asks that you do not venture into the palms as the natives seem unusually restless...*"
Norris cartoon reprinted from *Vancouver Sun* by permission of Stuart Keate, Publisher

It was at this time the multi-million dollar renovation of the hotel commenced. The very name "Operation Teacup" suggested a somewhat genteel onslaught. But the changes brought new life around the Inner Harbor without interfering with afternoon tea in the Empress lobby.

In November, 1968, Leslie Parkinson retired and something fresh was introduced to The Empress in the person of a new general manager, Louis J. Finamore. Formerly one of Hilton's key men, Finamore took over general supervision of CP Hotels in Calgary, Lake Louise, Banff and The Empress. He personified the "new look" in hoteliers while drawing on a lengthy experience in every feature of operating a modern hotel. It was not long before the hotel's purchasing department was ordering black ink instead of red for the accountants.

However, greater challenges beckoned Finamore and in the spring of 1973 the general managership of The Empress was handed over to William A. Gray, a long-time CP Hotels man, largely involved with marketing and sales. Gray had previously managed the chain's Hotel Saskatchewan, in Regina. In May, 1975, he returned to marketing and the general manager's office was occupied by E.G. (Ted) Balderson.

The hotel's busy season was just starting and Balderson had little opportunity to discover some of the old lady's idiosyncrasies. However, experience counts and Ted Balderson knew hotels from stock room to executive suite. In fact he started his career with CP Hotels in the stock room of the Banff Springs Hotel, and in 1971 he had the satisfaction of returning to that hotel as manager.

For 16 years "Mr B" steered the hotel through more ongoing refurbishings which, in effect had to be partially band-aid again, but he still found time to play an important part in organizations of public concern such as hospitals, charities and tourism promotion. In 1987 he transferred to Halifax but his keen interest and affection for The Empress brings him back to Victoria whenever an opportunity occurs.

In 1987 Mr. Ian Barbour was brought in as General Manager and given the job of overseeing the massive renovation and interconnection of the hotel with the Victoria Conference Centre. Barbour, a young Scotsman, with six years experience in Canada for the Four Seasons Hotel group, had by then got his renovation muscles fine tuned after developing and opening Vancouver's Mandarin Hotel. But more on his gargantuan task in a future chapter.

As with so many big hotels serving the public, little thought had been put to keeping records of their own achievements or those of the many dedicated men and women who have devoted years of their lives to the hospitality business. The Empress, through numerous chefs de cuisine, maitre d's, assistant managers and down through the ranks of bell hops, built up an international reputation for service and superb food. For many years maitre d'hotel Zanichelli guarded The Empress' reputation. He could look back on many years of unique experience attending to the wishes of royalty and commoner alike. With the CPR hotel system since 1927, when he first came to Canada he had to start as a busboy despite his considerable experience in the food profession. He could not speak a word of English and the customers at the old Hotel Vancouver, where he first worked in Canada, could not speak his native Italian or the French or Spanish in which he was fluent. Under the Vancouver's maitre d', James Kemp, Zanichelli prospered and ultimately succeeded his master in the same position. It was many years later after working in New York and at major eastern Canadian hotels that he came to The Empress.

There are dozens of loyal employees who have spent years of their lives at The Empress. Many came from other hotels in the chain while others have lived a lifetime in Victoria even taking over jobs previously held by their fathers. Eric Penty spent many years as supervisor of maintenance, his father had been the original chief engineer. Art Sanders ruled over the famous Empress gardens and greenhouses for over 26 years.

Don Wakelin started as an elevator boy at CPR's Royal York, in Toronto, in 1936, and spent almost 12 years as executive assistant manager of The Empress. Hall porter Lloyd Strickland joined the staff in 1939, went to war, came back and again hustled guests' baggage. Jimmie James, hotel valet for almost 30 years, kept the guests neat and tidy. Tommy Johnson, who dispensed his own particular brand of good cheer in the Bengal Room, joined the staff in May, 1929, and decided to retire, 50 years later, in 1979.

At one period The Empress dining room was staffed with waitresses. Ruby Holt, Lorraine Haslam, Dorothy Leadly and

Elsie Connon looked back on many continuous years of serving famous personalities and just plain folks with the same courtesy and efficiency in the dining room, the Garden Cafe and afternoon tea in the lobby.

Romance has not been confined to the hotel guests. Hall porter Bob Riddler, who started with the hotel in 1933, tried shipbuilding for three years, returned to the hotel in 1945 and married one of the maids, Margaret Sheline. During the stay of Princess Margaret at The Empress, in 1958, Margaret Riddler had the honor of attending the Princess. Len West started in the hotel kitchen, became doorman complete in plum colored frock-coat and married another Margaret, a pretty girl from the housekeeping staff.

A guest relaxing on one of the hotel's ornate couches can thank Elmer Hammer for its comfort and beautiful condition. Elmer was upholsterer for 30 years, refurbishing a continuous stream of Edwardian settees, armchairs and love seats. One-time Head Porter, Clem Michaels, was passing through Victoria early in 1959, but stopped to take a bell-hop job and stayed on for more than 20 years. When it came to keeping all The Empress wires uncrossed, Alex Jurens worked through 30 years of DC and AC current. As hotel electrician, he knew every switch and socket. Wilf Brown, head painter, must have painted the whole of the inside of the hotel at least half a dozen times since he started in 1948. Fred Bursey was Chief Engineer for many years and actually received a special award for the Most Exceptional Employee of the Year, an unheard of accomplishment for someone in a management position. So many of these dedicated workers have now retired and many have passed away, but it is the personalities of these and many more people who have imbued The Empress with its aura of class and unruffled service thereby assisting mightily in creating its reputation as one of the great hotels of our time.

Elizabethan-garbed carol singers are a feature of Empress Christmas festivities.

chapter 9

The First Christmas

By Ainslie Helmcken

Ainslie Helmcken was the grandson of the celebrated British Columbia doctor and legislator Hon. Dr. John Sebastian Helmcken: 1824-1920.

Having lived most of his life in Victoria, Ainslie Helmcken was THE authority on Victoriana, and with a rare touch of logic the City of Victoria appointed him official Archivist in 1966. Ainslie died in 1987.

Before the turn of the century Victoria was famed in many lands for the beauty of its site, its gardens, the parliament buildings, Roger's Chocolates, but few man-made pieces of construction.

Then came the fulfilment of many an abortive attempt to improve the harbor. With the reclamation of the "Mud Flats" a term by which James Bay was held in derision by one and all including the city council, things began to improve. The beautiful granite stone causeway emerged from the mud and general confusion of the area.

But how could this magnificent building, slowly climbing to the sky, be that which was destined to change, in time, the whole social structure of Victoria?

As a child and then as a small boy I had watched the progress of this work with wonderment but really not appreciating its true meaning. That all changed however in my first visit to the Empress Hotel on the very first day it was opened to the public. You see, Uncle Harry, he was Harry Dalls Helmcken, K.D., and himself a very well-liked native son, and his wife were moving into residence in the hotel and there were packages to be carried from their former residence in the old Driard Hotel and I was lucky enough to be a package carrier. The Harry Helmckens became very popular with other residents of The Empress and particularly with the staff as we shall see.

Just how the opening of The Empress made so many changes in the lives of many hostesses of the city can be seen in the social columns of the newspapers of that day. First a small advertisement which appeared in different forms in the newspapers telling the ladies how much they would enjoy entertaining in the Palm Room, that if you required the whole room the hotel would be glad to arrange it. Thereafter, by degrees, the "day at home" gradually lessened in favor of a large afternoon tea in the Palm Room.

Then of course there were the great balls, all of which were given much space, names of those present and descriptions of the ball gowns, all of which appeared in the press.

But it is of Christmas 1908, The Empress' first festive season, that this veritable wonderland impressed beyond description this small boy. That it was Boxing Day before I saw it in no way lessened the thrill.

"Empress Scene of Brilliant Ball."

"Employees of Hostelry Enjoy Evening with Many of the Friends."

Guests to the number of 700 had been invited; all the names were in the press report.

But what was this? Uncle Harry was Santa Claus? Really not a new role for him, he was Santa Claus to many all the year. But let's read a little further. Ah ha. Mrs. Harry had her finger in the pie. Yes she and Uncle Harry had provided a gift for nearly all the members of the staff and these were under the Christmas tree.

Since the ballroom was not built until later, all balls were at this time held in the rotunda (now known as the lobby). Great festoons of cedar and fir boughs decorated the pillars and walls. In the centre of the great room was the Christmas tree. At midnight, what must have been one of the first electrically illuminated trees in Victoria was turned on. Three hundred electric lights, DC power supplied from The Empress' own power plant, heralded the arrival of Christmas. A truly beautiful party. The Palm Room had been turned into a sitting room as was the practice for all great balls.

Now why didn't I see it on Christmas Day? This bothered me until I remembered that Christmas Day 1908 will never be forgotten, in the weather records at least, as one of the stormiest days in Victoria's history. Even the weather bureau was blown off the roof of the Post Office building! Nobody ventured out until we had to all pile into a hack to travel to Grandfather's for Christmas dinner. Uncle Harry and wife were there, as were all members of the family. One family The Empress had not changed - at least not that year.

In this modern era Victoria is still famed in many lands for the beauty of its site, its gardens, the parliament buildings, Roger's Chocolates. But now add the Dominion Astrophysical Observatory, Butchart Gardens, sport fishing and, of course, The Empress and even Christmas at The Empress.

Ever since Ainslie Helmcken's experience of the first Christmas at the hotel this annual celebration has been something special at The Empress. It was not until some years later that "Christmas At The Empress" took on its present medieval pageantry. In 1975 *Time* correspondent Jame Wilde, after attending preparations for the five day festival wrote:

"For 55 years it's "Annual Old English Yule Tide Festival" has been a rite of season's passage on which neither world war nor depression nor energy crisis has ever intruded. Many guests make an annual pilgrimage to take part in the celebration, which has become as much of an institution as, well, afternoon tea in The Empress' lobby."

Things get under way early on Christmas Day when madrigal singers dressed in the silks and velvets of Elizabethan costumes wake the thousand or so guests in the hotel with medieval carols as they pass down the corridors of six floors.

The spacious lobby of the hotel is heavy with the scent of cedar and pine boughs. There are snowberries, holly and scarlet poinsettias from the hotel's own greenhouses. A giant Christmas tree towers over the daily ceremony of afternoon tea.

In the early evening guests assemble in the lobby as the Yule Log is ceremonially dragged in by a procession headed by a cartwheeling jester in red and green tunic, cap and bells. Following closely come the trumpeter, in Tudor garb, and the stately seneschal who in stentorious tones, reads the Christmas proclamation. The Yule Log is planted in the fireplace and fired by an important personage with a splinter kept from the log of the previous year. Legend has it that if a Yule Log splinter is saved and kept under a bed until next Yuletide, no fire, crime or danger of any sort will come near the building for the next twelve months. Records do not state under whose bed the splinter is kept at The Empress.

Now comes the seignorial feast of over three tons of turkey and 1,200 pounds of plum pudding washed down with several thousand dollars worth of festive wines and liquors all contributing to what many people believe a traditional Christmas should be like.

The seven course Empress banquet is a mixture of Tudor magnificence and Edwardian elegance highlighted, soon after the fish course, with the Boar's Head procession. Here the "lord of the demesne", the Steward and seneschal or major-domo lead the various officers of a great baronial establishment, together with choristers giving thanks in carol and canticle.

Each succeeding course is conveyed into the dining rooms in procession culminating with 100 pound flaming Christmas puddings. "Wassail" cry the diners, although what they call by that name now would probably make an Elizabethan weep in his beard. The madrigal singers close the evening in song, often joined by well-fortified guests.

But the ceremonies are not over yet. Boxing Day, the day after Christmas, is an important holiday also. In England, where in medieval times the monks of certain orders would offer Mass for the safety of ships, a small box was placed on each vessel for contributions from the sailors.

Carrying a box from door to door to collect "Christmas Money" and gifts was an old custom also, and from that grew the present alms boxes which are placed in the English churches. These were opened on Boxing Day and their contents distributed among the poor of the parish.

At The Empress there are no alms boxes but gifts and donations are made to the less fortunate in other ways.

Boxing Day also serves hotel guests as a time for recuperation after a surfeit of merrymaking.

Main lounge of the Vice Regal suite (above) on the second floor in 1970. (Below) The Bridal Suite, in the same year.

chapter 10

From Other Pens

Over the years Vancouver Island, Victoria and The Empress have been the subjects of countless stories and articles. A few selected items follow:

From Earl Grey, Governor General of Canada, 1908.

There is a saying which is attributed to Princess Louise, who is reported after her arrival at Victoria to have cabled Her Majesty, the late Queen Victoria, that British Columbia was half-way between Balmoral and Heaven.

I hope I may not be considered guilty of an extravagance when I say that when the other evening I drifted quietly past your archipelago of lovely islands, and gazed upon the unruffled surface of your narrow waters, which reflected the surrounding mountains in their depths, I felt, in the quiet and dreamy atmosphere of the wonderful scenery, only broken by the plunge of the salmon and by the strings of duck necklacing the lovely bosoms of your bays, that Princess Louise had erred in not having located your province even nearer to heaven than she did.

From Barry Mather, a British Columbia writer, 1958.

A million years ago all of what is now British Columbia was covered with ice. Victoria is the only place that never

The large room in the lower lobby was an English-style pub until prohibition forced its closure. It has since become the more conventional Georgian Lounge and was once the scene of the final playoff of a golf tournament when sudden snow blanketed local golf courses.

thawed out....It is also known as the Mecca where elderly people visit their grandparents.

From Mrs. Agnes Rothery, a traveller from the United States, 1943.

Everyone on Government Street is strolling...the horses are drowsing by the curb; dogs are asleep in the doorways; a fat tabby cat washes her face with meditative deliberation. It is all rather like a retarded motion-picture film.

One of the advantages is that there is plenty of time to look at people: at the white-moustached, ruddy-cheeked gentleman in the good old tweed coat, carrying the good old pipe and swinging the good old cane at the dowager in long jet earrings, sweeping hat, and - actually in this year of our Lord - a feather boa.

Victoria has long been the Resort Perfect. It has offered climate, scenery, history and just enough retired diplomats and bronzed army and navy officers - to say nothing of elegant or shabby gentlemen of leisure - to blow a cosmopolitan air through the atmosphere of cosy confinement....Hollywood actors and actresses like to do what they call rusticate in the lofty salons, the dining room hung with portraits of British royalty, the conservatory of The Empress that is a perfumed epitome of the changing seasons.

Producers, with all their galaxy of stars and starlets, directors, photographers, wardrobe mistresses, publicity men, have used the nearby fjord scenery for moving pictures presumably set in Norway. Sometimes, with all such comings and goings, Victoria has seemed not so much like a little bit of England as a little bit of Hollywood.

From Ellery Littleton, A British Columbia columnist.

"I suspect that Victoria is the only Canadian city where a British, or pseudo-British, accent is widely accepted as normal and unremarkable. Working-class British accents carry no more clout here than they do in England. What counts is the style and sounds of the upper and upper-middle class: The blazers and flannels, tweeds and caps, gin and tonics, the iced tea tinkling in the shade beside the cricket pitch....It is redfaces and shouting at the rugger match, slightly aged sports cars, golf shoes in the hall-closet, and a certain bluff and hearty haw-haw hello."

From Dorothy Wrotnowski. For many years a columnist with The Victoria Colonist, *she covered The Empress Hotel.*

"My first impression of The Empress Hotel was glorious - the stuff that dreams are made of - and has stayed with me all through the years. It was back in the mid-twenties when three British naval ships visited Victoria for a few days. I only remember the name of one, *H.M.S. Hood.*

I was down from Duncan staying with friends so was in on many of the activities arranged for the visitors. The night before the ships were to sail there was a ball at The Empress. At age 16, I was most definitely not allowed to attend dances. But the couple with whom I was staying insisted. It didn't take much persuasion (mother wasn't there).

So in borrowed finery of orchid crepe de chine and silver lace I was ready for the ball, and that is an understatement.

Hardly inside the door and I was waltzing around the room and never stopped all evening. Bands playing, good-looking men in naval uniforms and soon the evening passed in a dream. Heady stuff for a 16 year old. That evening also set a standard for manners that I thought men should have.

The Empress has never lost the charm of that first evening, not in all the years I have covered events and people in the hotel. And it never will.

At the Christmas family dinner one year I took my mother, son, and my two grandchildren to the festive party. Like all children when excited there were trips to the washroom. Taking young Paula to the Ladies Room, half way up the stairs near the dining room - the one with the beautiful oak door - on entering, Paula became quite wide-eyed, asking "Was this really a washroom?" On affirmation she said "Well, this is nicer than a lot of living rooms".

From Prime Minister Mackenzie King, in Ottawa.

"No one knows anything of British Columbia."

[Many British Columbian's feel this opinion still persists in Ottawa today]

Room 164 (above) as it appears in 1908 and room 230 (below) in the early 1930's.

chapter 11

Operation Teacup - 1966

"Good Heavens Prudence They are changing The Empress"

Times change and time caught up with The Empress. Her owners, The Canadian Pacific Railway Company, had been worrying for years over the outdated plumbing, antiquated power supply, abnormal cost of operation and quantity of red ink required to record the fiscal situation.

When the Company threatened to raze the building and perhaps erect something more in keeping with today, the citizens of Victoria and the press cried, "Don't you dare!" *The San Francisco Examiner* even headlined "O Tempora, O Mores, Oh Please".

It would seem someone up there at Canadian Pacific headquarters must have read the papers or heard these exhortations because a number of experts in construction and hotel operation were called in to make extensive surveys to determine just what should be done.

Meanwhile the citizens of Victoria and Empress lovers all over the continent waited anxiously. One newspaper kernalled the situation with the headline "Victoria's Grand Old Lady Calmly Awaits Diagnosis." Letters poured through the press. Even the Premier of British Columbia, W.A.C. Bennett, brought pressure to bear. A high government official came out bluntly and perhaps maliciously with "The Empress is disintegrating," while columnist, Herb Caen of San Francisco quoted someone as saying, "I like old things, but there is such a thing as too old."

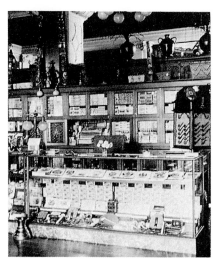

Room number 463 (below) after Operation Teacup in 1968. The original cigar stand (above) in the lobby has now been replaced in a more commodious setting on the lower main floor adjacent to the Garden Cafe.

It was June of 1966 when a sigh of relief swept across the Strait of Georgia, over the Rockies and prairies and into the directors' lounge of the railway company. The decision to spend four million dollars on giving the old lady a major surgical operation was the greatest news Victorians had received since Kitchener relieved Khartoum.

Again the press came out with headlines. *The Financial Times* "A New Grasp On Life For Famous Empress." *Ottawa Journal*, "It's Crumpets As Usual." *The Canadian*, "Good Heavens Prudence They're Changing The Empress," and the *New York Times* noted "A Grand Hotel Switches Its Current."

Nevertheless, and in spite of official pronouncements, there were some misgivings among the natives. To calm their fears, management very quickly issued a statement: "Afternoon tea will definitely not be suspended during alterations." As a further balm for apprehensive nerves, plans were even discussed to renovate the musical trio and put it back in the lobby to help the tea go down.

This four million dollar renovation scheme was dubbed "Operation Teacup", but just as the estimates for the construction of the original hotel skyrocketed, so the cost of "Operation Teacup" almost doubled, and in a way, has become something of a continuing campaign.

Once it was decided to raise the hemline and freshen the old lady's make-up with some swinging innovations it was considered prudent to concentrate on providing 270 up-to-date rooms with modern service to match while retaining and even enhancing the traditional aura of a cultivated corner of England that has helped to make the hotel famous.

The first public unveiling of the new look in The Empress was the opening of the Garden Cafe, formerly known by the prosaic name of the Coffee Shop. That initial introduction to the "new" Empress suggested the old lady of Government Street had plenty of life left in her.

Much of "Operation Teacup" was concerned with a trimming of the hotel to present-day standards with such amenities as an efficient heating system, AC electric current instead of the homemade brand of DC and the provision of TV sets and air conditioning. The Douglas Street parking lot was enlarged, but the wooden trelliswork down the middle, placed there when the

The first addition to the hotel was built in 1912 and included the Reading Room. (Below) The same room, now The Bengal Room, which succeeded the Coronation Lounge in 1967.

The famous Empress Dining Room as it appeared on opening day January 20, 1908. (Below) The same dining room was renovated during Operation Teacup in 1967.

The Elizabethan Room was originally used as a writing room. In 1967 after a spell as an antique shop, it became the Library Bar (below). The hand painted ceiling is a masterpiece and the room is now a gallery for Native arts.

hotel opened, was retained. The vice-regal or royal suite was re-located close to the new automatic elevators at a cost of $50,000.

Other major improvements included redesigning the kitchens with installation of a great deal of new equipment, and the demolition of the old power house and laundry, with its tall chimney, on the far side of Douglas Street.

This aspect of facelifting had its own problems, since it must be completed with the least possible disturbance to guests. The massive job employed 175 local men and the daily bill for materials bought locally ran between $2,000 and $3,000.

This streamlining surgery was only part of the problem. Fittings and furniture caused headaches too!

Approximately 22,000 feet of carpeting had to be acquired, (that is over four miles) then hoisted by crane through windows on each floor. Four tapestries were specially woven in Vancouver and placed on the walls of the Garden Cafe. Bedspreads for 600 new six-foot-six beds were specially loomed. (To illustrate the expense of running a first class hotel those same bedspreads have since been replaced twice.)

Some 1,200 pieces of furniture were specifically designed to fit into existing decor and another 2,000 pieces re-upholstered, much of it done in the hotel's own shop. Then there was the business of antiques.

Though not all existing furniture is the real thing, there are nevertheless many items of genuine lineage such as authentic hand-carved Chippendale tables, plus chairs and tables of the English Renaissance and Regency periods.

Two sideboards, Louis XIV style, were restored by a wood sculptor and artist from Hungary, with materials brought in from Paris and Italy. Solid oak refectory tables of early Elizabethan vintage would take four men to lift. Open the doors of some old chests and the aroma is of centuries and of vinegar mixed with honey.

Numerous solid brass chandeliers would fetch hundreds of dollars each in today's market...if you could find them. Otherwise the inventory included far more than 5,000 chairs and 12,000 pieces of furniture that had to be catalogued to determine if they were of genuine Empress era. Those that were not were disposed of and replaced with items obtained from other hotels and antique

The original Crystal Ballroom (above) was added in 1914. It has undergone several redecorations (below) since then, but none to compare with the 1989 restoration (see color section).

dealers throughout the world. All this developed into something of a furniture hunt, for it was determined to have nothing fake in The Empress. It also turned into something of a bonanza for Victorians who snapped up old-fashioned light fittings, beds, carpet, drapes and kitchen equipment. One local had his antique Cadillac fitted with carpet bearing the royal crown pattern from the old Coronet lounge.

One noteworthy piece of furniture is the grandfather clock, securely attached to a pillar in the main lobby. This is a genuine Sheraton and to this day an accurate timekeeper. An interested visitor from Texas once had his offer of $10,000 courteously declined. There is another, older Chippendale grandfather clock in one of the private suites.

Those carrying out the refurbishing had a lot to work with. There were the original three-inch-thick solid oak doors, some old washbasins you could stand in, spitoons in the barber's shop, and the original three-foot-diameter crystal lights in the ballroom. Then there were silverware, cutlery, and chinaware, paintings, prints and portraits, some of which would be impossible to procure nowadays. These by themselves are worth a mint of money.

Judging by the enthusiasm and calibre of the people who guided "Operation Teacup" it had to be a success. But one official remarked "We can't afford to make mistakes, we have too many "Empressarios" looking over our shoulders!"

The Palm Room was the centre of all formal gatherings in the early days of the hotel. The Crystal Ballroom was added to the left of the picture in 1914.

chapter 12

A ROYAL
RESTORATION

"The multi-million dollar expert restoration has enhanced the beauty of the 81 year old Victoria heritage landmark, increased the stately hotel's charming character and updated its hotel services."

Robert S. De Mone, President Canadian Pacific Hotels

"We're going to do the job and we're going to do it right, we're not going to cut back on the scope or the quality of the work; we will pay what it takes." With this memo from Head Office on his desk, The Empress Hotel's new General Manager, Ian Barbour, embarked on the most extensive and costly restoration of a hotel in Canada.

There is a curious mystique about Victoria and The Empress. Barbour was quick to atune to these vibes when he arrived in 1987, realizing the changes and improvements were going to be closely monitored by many who still treasured the old girl.

"A very important element", he said, "was uppermost in our minds when we were planning the work. There was to be no question that we must maintain the architectural integrity of the original building and the character of its contents."

Back in the 1960's The Empress had experienced something of a restoration, or healing to the tune of $6 million. But come the 80's with the significant increase in international travel, expansion of tourism and demand for quality in hospitality services, what had once been a top-notch hotel was again looking a little dowdy despite its outstanding architecture and wonderful site. There were difficulties in competing with the new hotels and restaurants nearby; their owners always passing on the way to the bank.

Already in the works at Canadian Pacific headquarters was the formation of a Master Plan. A team of very skilled architects and space planners interviewed people in the Pacific area and those in the hospitality industry within the company.

What do you want it to be, what's adequate or not, what's too big or small? An incredibly thorough examination. How big should the laundry be? How many seats in the employees' cafeteria? New approaches to the new entrance?

Emphasis must be placed on the historical perspectives and don't forget the Victorians. "The Empress is their hotel", they say.

Some things which had to be improved stood out boldly. The lobby - totally inadequate to handle summer volume plus the inconvenience for guests staying in the hotel or even trying to register while afternoon tea seekers tumbled over departing guests' luggage. A new reception area with more elevators is a first priority.

And while the builders are at it the often considered swimming pool and health club must be added.

Now as to quality. This must be tops. A total commitment to quality must never be questioned. In design, construction, furnishings, restorative work, decorating, everything both public area and behind the scenes, must reach perfection.

There was much discussion on scheduling. When and how can it be done? Over a few years without closing the hotel? But the most expedient and effective way was to shut it down. A decision of great concern for any business to make.

The Empress has a significant economic influence on Southern Vancouver Island through staff members and their families, suppliers and service companies. A winter closure made sense for many reasons.

In December 1987, a year before the closure, 300 suppliers and media were provided with an information kit outlining the plan so they could prepare for a long hiatus without The Empress' business.

Suggestions were made to help alleviate as much disturbance as possible such as closing parts of plants for any necessary restorations or sending staff on winter vacations, or to other Canadian Pacific hotels.

October 23rd, 1988 the doors closed for the second time in the hotel's history. This October closing was for just under six months. The doors had to re-open April 12th, 1989. And they did!

Many suppliers did not fully realize how much Empress business affected them until the closure. As Ian Barbour remarked "A lot of local people were around to shake my hand when we were back in business saying 'did we ever miss you'. This included taxi drivers, bus operators, retailers and suppliers. And for that matter almost everyone in Victoria".

During the six months' round the clock activity, the project employed well over 500 full-time workers apart from specific hotel staff, and indirectly, a further 1,500.

The extensive front lawns of the hotel, famous for various events, demonstrations and even a tennis match between Bobby Riggs and members of the British Columbia legislature, were decimated with quantities of gravel spread for several trailer trucks and portable buildings for electricians' and plumbers' tools and supplies.

The gardens were protected by heavy wire mesh spread on the lawns for more car parking.

The whole operation was a hard hat area for everyone permitted on the site.

There was concern that tradesmen capable of undertaking much of the necessary detailed work, would be difficult to find and lure to Victoria. But happily, because it was Victoria, it was less a problem than imagined. Many tradesmen on Vancouver Island were older and still had the kinds of skills needed in terms of furniture re-finishing, or hand building the beautiful capitals and plaster mouldings atop the many pillars.

Plasterers were working five months doing nothing but making mouldings such as can be seen in the magnificently recreated work around the beautiful Palm Court.

At least 70 percent of the original splendour, damaged or destroyed over the years, was replaced by craftsmen using skills they had not had the opportunity to use for years. Two of these artisans came out of retirement especially to be a part of the exciting venture.

Many workers applied just for the experience, while others had worked on renovations at the hotel before and wanted the opportunity to practice dormant skills uncalled for in the modern chrome and plastic era.

Talented carpenters and refinishers also played a major role in many parts of the great scheme.

Every single door from over 400 rooms was tagged with its room number, removed, stripped, refinished and fitted with new solid brass handles and locks and their heavy brass hinges, weighing 2 lbs, replaced. Each door only fitted its particular frame, which emphasized the original quality craftsmanship. Mouldings around each of these doors were made up of 28 pieces of wood. Someone worked out up to 12 miles of moulding went into the restoration.

The hotel's main lobby had been fully carpeted for many years. Following the overall plan of inspecting all details of construction to assess conditions of soundness, it was decided to strip all the carpet from the lobby floor for inspection.

Imagine the surprise and pleasure experienced when a magnificent inlaid hardwood floor was exposed. It's only blemishes being thousands of carpet-tacks and staples. A gang of knee-capped extricators working over many hours removed every nail, tack and staple, and experts then refinished the floor to its original beauty.

The Palm Court in the early days before the Crystal Ballroom was built, in 1914, was the show place of the hotel. Here tea was served beneath the beautiful stained glass dome. This dome had similar accoustic peculiarities as the great dome of London's St. Paul's Cathedral with its whispering gallery. Words whispered on one side of the room could be distinctly heard on the other side.

At the time of Operation Teacup the priceless dome was badly damaged by an unusually heavy snowfall and replaced with a roof suitably plastered inside.

The Royal Restoration plan, however, specifically called for complete replacement of a magnificent stained glass dome and all the intricate artistic plaster work.

The well known Crystal Ballroom was, of course, completely restored. Originally it had an unusual glass ceiling. But modern visual equipment for meetings doesn't want sunshine interfering. So the glass was replaced with mirror providing a delightfully different atmosphere. An exquisitely patterned carpet from England covers the entire floor and if there is a need for dancing, a portable parquet floor is placed over the carpet.

The ten crystal chandeliers were lowered and completely taken apart. Each piece washed and hand polished then re-strung and re-hung. A very costly and time consuming operation.

One workman engaged on this delicate job recalled how, as a young man, he had been involved with the cleaning of the fragile and expensive chandeliers during the Operation Teacup.

"We built a wood device on the back of a pick-up truck. Hung a chandelier on the wood rack, made it fast with bailing wire and drove the pick-up through a car wash. Several times for each chandelier." Which brings to mind Ian Barbour's remarks about doing it right, whatever the cost.

Guests now enter to register in a new building towards the northwest corner. There was some critical comment about the design, but when the weather, and maybe a little Empress ivy, have found the new stone facing and a year's maturity, people will forget the old port cochere at the south end.

There are now 480 guest rooms, 60 more than when the hotel closed in 1988. These guest rooms reflect a high standard of beauty and luxury. Calgary Interior Decorator, Kerry Busby, selected for each room a functional yet beautifully crafted armoire containing a large TV with remote, a mini-bar and space for guests' clothing, et cetera. Matching bedside cabinets and rich colours for drapes, bedspreads and carpets together with restored antique accents delight hotel guests. Ten million dollars were spent on furnishings and three hundred thousand dollars on re-finishing existing Empress antique pieces.

The many public rooms and wide passageways were furnished and decorated by Deborah Lloyd-Forrest of Dallas. Deborah travelled far and wide for an impressive collection of artifacts to complement the Empress antiques which were all superbly refinished by local craftsmen.

The hotel has got its famous potted plants back. Now they are displaying their beauty in an array of exotic planters, jardinieres and giant Oriental urns.

The interesting collection of framed portraits of Canada's First Ladies, the wives of the Governors General, have been gracefully hung throughout the hotel's many hallways.

Basically The Empress operates on six floors. The seventh floor can only be reached by stairs. But since one of the most popular guest rooms is the Bridal Suite the Romantic Attic was conceived!

Eight beautiful rooms, specifically designed for honeymooners were prepared on the seventh floor up an easy private staircase. Grooms are not obliged to carry their brides up the stairs, but it is said one athletic type did just that.

The great dining room with its rich beamed ceiling and tall windows was one of the showplaces of the original hotel. However its very size made it a most difficult place to provide the high standard of service required by today's guests.

The great room has now been divided in half. The west-end overlooking the Inner Harbor has become an elegant lounge, extravagantly furnished and decorated for those wishing to take refreshment in luxury.

Across the centre passageway a splendid new dining room has been created, closer to the kitchens and furnished with excellent taste and just the right size of room for staff to offer peerless service. And the many "Empressarios" can rest happily the famous beamed ceiling is still intact and, if anything may be seen to better advantage.

The renowned Bengal Room has been cleverly upgraded and restored, yet its unique character has been retained, including the famous curry lunch buffet. The all-day Garden Cafe has also been completely redecorated to a more contemporary bistro style.

On the lower floor of the hotel, at the southwest end of the main corridors you will find a miniature museum. Old photographs, pieces of memorabelia, books and other archival items chronicle the hotel's past.

With all these, and dozens more activities striving to meet the deadline, hotel staff had to be trained for a whole new hotel.

Classrooms were set up in the adjoining Conference Centre where some 200 new and established employees were fully instructed in the finer points of The Empress service and attention to guests comfort. The scores of changes made throughout the many floors, passages and public rooms were visually introduced.

Some employees were dispatched to Florida to learn the intricacies of a modern computerized hotel operation. Computers were introduced to enhance the hotel service, not to reduce personalized attention. More than a hundred thousand dollars was spent on the importance of good training.

Even though the hotel was closed, preparation for the opening of the Victoria Conference Centre, on January 12, 1989, took precedence. All the catering services for this splendid new facility come under the hotel's stewardship so special kitchen areas were constructed in the centre and staffed by Empress employees. The extensive new Empress kitchens can also be involved when necessary.

The well known main lobby of the hotel has a new arrangement of excellent shops in the hallway leading through the conservatory to the impressive new Conference Centre.

Naturally afternoon tea will continue to be served in the lobby and in summer the Palm Court will also accommodate the tea and crumpet clientele under the dome.

On the west end of the Humboldt wing a glass enclosed Health Club has been added. Guests have the choice of immersing themselves in a 25 metre swimming pool, a large jacuzzi, or a ladies' or gentlemen's sauna. Joints and muscles can be tuned up in the large exercise room using will-power or a good selection of mechanical devices. There is also a wading pool for youngsters.

Just as nature played a trick on the hotel in 1928, when an underground stream caused problems joining the Humboldt wing to the main building, so nature entangled herself with the hotel in 1989.

When renovations began there was evidence that The Empress ivy was literally taking over sections of the building, growing into the walls, causing dampness and cracks. It was necessary to make a thorough survey of the problem.

For appearances some ivy had to be retained but there must also be a lot of pruning. An expert advisor was brought in from

England and set up a plan of attack to control and nurture the decorative problem.

An ivy root had to be removed from the southwest corner. A heavy digging machine tackled the job. After hours of work the machine won and the 60 square foot monster root was unearthed.

Two types of ivy grace some of the hotel's walls. The Boston variety is a little better behaved in that it sheds it's leaves and sleeps in winter while the English variety makes a nuisance of itself year round.

Parts of The Empress gardens had, from time to time, fallen to so called progress. Segments here and there, had been annexed for "Horrors!" a bus depot and increased parking. Greenhouses were dismantled. Fortunately a large section of the rose garden survived and enjoyed praise from visitors. The front of the hotel has always been kept immaculate. The Royal Restoration included work to enhance the rose garden. New shrubs and a beautiful arbor have been established on the south end and the lawns have been levelled.

At the northwest corner there is an area that has been developed into a quiet retreat with winding pathways, a bridge over a pond and a collection of rocks, plants and other vegetation indigenous to British Columbia.

Behind the scenes there were major improvements made in laundry, kitchen and storage facilities. The original public rooms at the rear of the lower floor were replaced with Personnel and Purchasing offices and a large new pastry kitchen and bake shop.

With 24 months' work to be completed in 6 months it was natural the scheduled re-opening date, early in April, was uppermost on a lot of minds. But Mother Nature had to take another whack at the royal edifice by presenting the coldest winter for several years. Outside work on the project was shut down for weeks.

The last days of March soon became April and the activity in, out and around the Empress accelerated to something bordering on a crescendo. If ever the foundations of the hotel were going to be tested this was it. Everything went ahead as slated.

Hotel management were so impressed with the personal interest and commitment of the work force, a party was organized for some 500 craftsmen, carpenters, electricians, in fact, all workers who contributed their skills to the monumental undertaking. This was not just a few beers, cheese and crackers. This was the real McCoy.

Guests were invited to bring their spouses. And all turned up in their individual finery. One party of plumbers and their ladies arrived in stretch limousines, the gentlemen suited in grey top hats and tails.

Not only was the party a whale of a success but it served as a trial run for the staff and a grand way to show management's appreciation for everyone's effort.

April 12th arrived all too soon but at 7.45 a.m. a guest arrived to register. He was immediately accommodated as booked and a steady stream of guests started to check in.

As the morning sun appeared round the sides of the building men were busy laying new turf where the original lawns had been trashed. Inside at various locations throughout the hotel carpenters and painters were busy putting final touches to this and that.

Afternoon tea was a sellout from the moment the first teabags luxuriated in the silver tea pots.

Guided tours of the new look were organized for the public from 10 a.m. to 9 p.m. during the first six weeks after re-opening and over 8,000 visitors enthused over the transformation.

As a special recognition of the importance of employees past and present, a Pride Delegation was formed for the May 24 Gala party and official reopening of the hotel. All present employees and all surviving retired employees of the hotel were invited as guests to the magnificent affair.

Tributes were paid, reminiscences exchanged and warm feeling of achievement helped to christen the elegant Crystal Ballroom. British Columbia's Lieutenant Governor David Lam as guest of honor, declared The Empress Royally Restored. Even Queen Victoria would have been amused!

The Reception Pavilion with wide paved driveways. Cars can be driven to underground parking at the left. Inside the pavilion guests can register in comfort and with easy access to elevators at the rear.

chapter 13

A Colorful Look At The Empress

"...a glimpse of the old dowager in her new finery!"

Not just a facelift but a total renovation, The Empress hotel was completely transformed during the Royal Restoration of 1989. Antique furnishings, richly colored carpets and rugs, decorative accents from many parts of the world and beautifully restored architectural features delight the guests and locals alike. The following pages offer a glimpse of the old dowager in her new finery!

The famous Empress plants have returned to the lobby in exotic oriental urns. The original lobby entrance to the Palm Room has been restored.

The original Palm Room has been completely restored to its former grandeur including the magnificent glass dome.

Many fine pieces of antique furniture have been tastefully displayed throughout the rooms and hallways, together with portraits of Royalty and the wives of Canada's Governors General.

The guest rooms have been furnished in colorful luxury.

The lobby has been completely refurnished with the accent on the serving of afternoon tea. The tall pillars have been restored to their original splendor.

The Bengal Room has added features onto its original theme but the famous curries have been retained by popular demand.

Once part of the dining room, the comfortable luxurious lounge features a view of the harbor and antique furnishings that complement the new dining room across the hall.

The original Empress dining room has been divided into two rooms one a lounge and the other a smaller, more inviting room for gourmet dining.

The Garden Cafe has been given a more bistro appearance.
At the northwest end of the hotel a modern health club has been added.
Swimming pool, jacuzzi, saunas, children's wading pool and the latest in
exercise machines are available for hotel guests.

*The Crystal Ballroom takes on the appearance of a fabulous film set.
The Empress is connected to the Victoria Conference Centre by a
walkway that once housed the famous conservatory.*

chapter 14

The Dowager Means Business

"Victoria is a tweedy, daffodilish, green-fingered sort of place, a golfish, fly-fishing, 5 o'clock teapot place..."

Bruce Hutchison

Because of their fond attitude towards The Empress, it has become easy for the majority of Victoria's residents to overlook the fact that this vine-covered pile, set in its manicured landscape is also a business that contributes considerably to the economy of the area. Victoria had always advertised itself as a tourist city but it may surprise people to learn that The Empress also spends well over a quarter of a million dollars yearly on promotion. Most of this campaign is angled in the general direction of the United States. That it pays off is demonstrated by the sharp increase in tourists who enjoy the sea trip from Seattle to Victoria on fast catamarans or ferries fitted with gambling machines. Of course, this influx benefits The Empress but these tourist dollars are not channeled to the coffers of the hotel exclusively because most of it is spent in restaurants, shops and tourist attractions throughout Victoria and the Island. In fact it has been said a dollar changes hands three times in the area, on the same day.

The summer tourist boom is obvious to everyone since its effect on the traffic in the streets, stores and sidewalks of Victoria takes on the dimensions of peaceful invasion almost obliterating the native inhabitants. Added to this influx of dollars are those spent by delegates to the numerous conventions held during the so-called off-season at The Empress and Victoria's fine new Conference Centre adjoining. All of which has come to make the shops specializing in woolens, china and other goods dear to the hearts of American visitors, certainly realize that these potential customers are a large part of their raison d'etre.

Of course not all the guests of the hotel are trippers from the United States. There is another group that shares this almost proprietory right to the amenities of gracious living. From the Prairies, they come to the Coast each winter, arousing the envy of the folks back home by sending postcards in which they describe such unheard of things as roses blooming outdoors in December. Having escaped blizzards and sub-zero temperatures in a most agreeable way, most of them return to their hometowns as spring advances. But they are as completely migratory as any swallow and, year after year, they are welcomed by The Empress as familiar winter guests.

The great increase in tourist air travel has also made it commonplace to overhear conversations in Japanese, German, French and other languages, including the several dialects from the United Kingdom, which perhaps rouse a ghost or two from the corridors of "...the old Pet of the British Empire".

With its regular staff of about 300 employees, The Empress must be considered as an important employer and here the permanence and stability of the enterprise is exemplified by the fact that 20, 30 and even 40 years of service are not uncommon. In the summer months, in order to cope with the tourist flood, an additional 200 young people are taken on staff, most of them university students using their vacation time to finance their education.

Over the last few years great changes have taken place in the hotel industry. The complexity of operation with all its interlocking services and departments, has proved the value of courses in hotel management encompassing everything from accounting to catering and labor relations. It is a strange fact that in Europe the old tradition of management originating in the haute cuisine of the kitchen persists whereas on this continent it usually comes from the clerical staff.

Travelers today are much more sophisticated than even a few years ago, due no doubt to the greater mobility of our society. For example, it is not so long ago that one of the problems connected with attending to the wants of visitors from some of the more remote exotic lands was serving their national dishes. Such travelers found western foods strange and unappetizing. Now, however, this type of guest travels so extensively and so often that he has become perfectly accustomed to standard fare.

But although food is in the process of becoming standardized throughout the world, drinking water is not and the rapidity of jet transport with travelers visiting several widely separated countries in the space of a few days can mean disturbing stomach upsets from this source. As a result, the one specialty item that the Empress must stock for such world tourists is a bottled supply of chemically pure drinking water.

When they visit Victoria, high ranking guests of State often stay at Government House. Yet it is the usual custom during such visits to hold the official banquet in their honor at The Empress. If the visiting delegation is of any size, the accompanying members of the entourage live in the hotel and, in preparation for such special affairs, the menus are drawn up in great detail months in advance. Care must be taken to make sure selected ingredients of choice quality are on hand precisely when they are needed.

Another indication of the increased sophistication of today's traveler is the decrease in the number of articles removed by "souvenir seekers". At one time, people stayed in hotels so infrequently they were tempted to slip some small suitably inscribed article into their suitcase as proof to friends and family back home that they had, indeed, been guests in such plush surroundings.

At The Empress, even today there are those for whom this urge is overpowering and of the 1,300 bath towels that must be replaced at The Empress each year, only 300 wear out while the remaining 1,000 apparently end up in the bathrooms of private homes. Coffee spoons are another favorite souvenir and they disappear at the rate of over 2,000 a year. However, as noted, this kind of pilfering is on the wane with the bulk of today's more sophisticated and knowledgeable travelers far beyond the "Oh-gee-whiz-look-where-I've-been" stage.

The Empress with its 1912 addition at right. The famous ivy is already creeping up a corner. Note the street cars, the forerunners of today's imported London buses. (Below) A few years later and the ivy is creeping wider and higher.

At one time, most of the buying for CPR hotels was done by a main purchasing department in Eastern Canada and shipped to the various locations. Nowadays, the policy is that everything possible will be bought locally and this, of course, is another considerable boon to Victoria's economy. Consider, for instance, that The Empress kitchens use about 60,000 pounds of butter each year and approximately 60,000 dozen eggs in the same period. That must mean something to the butter and egg man. Meat is not such a big item on The Empress menu as it used to be. Sufficient to say, though, a sizeable herd is consumed over the year. Salmon, always popular with visitors to the Coast, runs to about 1,500 pounds a month. If it takes 8,000 cucumbers a year for sandwiches, salads and garnishing imagine the quanitity of onions and potatoes which have to be peeled. Quite a sizeable grocery bill.

Don't let us overlook that indispensable accompaniment to "Afternoon Tea in the Lobby" - the Crumpet, an English gastronomic oddity the Oxford dictionary describes as a "soft cake of flour, eggs and milk". Soft? Cake? Well, no matter, They are delicious when one's appetite is hearty and certainly are popular since about 100,000 of the pastey tasties pass through the kitchens every year. One can only assume that they are, indeed, eaten but the same goes for 100,000 scones, all baked in the hotel's wonderful new pastry shop.

Apart from such quantities of supplies that contribute so much to the shops and wholesalers of Victoria, there are smaller expenditures among the skilled professionals who are unfortunately disappearing from the modern scene. The Empress has three grand pianos and four uprights which must be kept in tune and the piano tuner makes a regular monthly visit to ensure that the various clubs and parties who meet there will have proper accompaniment to their revels.

Also, it can happen occasionally that some exuberant guest will test the effects of strong drink on the inner workings of these instruments and then an emergency call to the piano tuner is necessary to prevent the onset of whiskey voice in the keyboard.

And so it goes. From laundry to lamb chops, champagne to salt shakers, the purchasing department shells out its largesse from day to day while plumbers and painters, cleaners and clerks

The hotel in 1975 with the new lower level walkway. The ivy, here in complete control, was tamed in 1989. A massive ivy root was excavated at the front right corner.

work around the clock to keep this hive of activity moving smoothly at a subdued hum.

Suffice to say The Empress is to Victoria what Victoria is to The Empress. The two are inseparable and such misguided people who might strive to do away with the charm of this famous hotel and change the character of Victoria to that of a buzzing metropolis, would better themselves by moving to other areas. This quiet soft-climated city will never be a racy raucous town and The Empress will always be a show place of elegance and dignity, qualities which perhaps stun and frighten those who have lost, or never had, either couth or cool. For those who possess both, The Empress and Victoria usually turn out to be something of an Edwardian Shangri-la which must be revisited time and time again.

Why?

Because more than just once, both of them have to be seen to be believed.

The Author.

Born in Sussex, England, Godfrey Holloway has spent some 38 years in Canada - and most of his life - connected with the stage, films, radio, televison and writing. In 1930 he toured Alberta's Peace River country with a Chautaqua tent show, acted in radio plays for CKUA, Edmonton, and was one of the founders of the Edmonton Little Theatre.

In 1931, Holloway journeyed back to England where utilizing his varied talents as a writer, actor and stage manager, he continued his professional career in London's West End theatre world and with the BBC. Later he moved to France to manage international radio stations beaming commercial programmes into the United Kingdom. With the outbreak of World War II, Holloway operated the freedom radio stations from France for Czechoslovakia and Austria. After the French capitulation, it was once more to England where, as Production Controller for the Combined Services Radio Unit, he worked with many Canadians and most of the famous entertainers of the day.

In 1951, Holloway returned to Canada with his wife and family. Since then he has set up the radio and television department for a major advertising agency and produced several award-winning TV commercials and documentary films.

Now retired, Godfrey Holloway lives with his wife on Vancouver Island.